Classical Greek Models of the Gospels and Acts

Studies in Mimesis Criticism

Classical Greek Models of the Gospels and Acts

Studies in Mimesis Criticism

*Edited by Mark G. Bilby, Michael Kochenash,
& Margaret Froelich*

Claremont Studies in New Testament
and Christian Origins 3

Classical Greek Models of the Gospels and Acts
Studies in Mimesis Criticism
Edited by Mark G. Bilby, Michael Kochenash, and Margaret Froelich
©2018 Claremont Press
1325 N. College Ave
Claremont, CA 91711

ISBN: 978-1-946230-18-8

Library of Congress Cataloging-in-Publication Data

Classical Greek Models of the Gospels and Acts: Studies in Mimesis Criticism/Edited by Mark G. Bilby, Michael Kochenash, and Margaret Froelich
    xiv + 187 pp. 22 x 15 cm. –(Claremont Studies in New Testament and Christian Origins 3)
    Includes bibliographical references and index.
    ISBN: 978-1-946230-18-8
    1.   Bible. N.T. Gospels — Criticism, interpretation, etc.
    2.   Bible. N.T. Acts-- Criticism, interpretation, etc.

BS 2548 C62 2018

Cover: Monument Sculpture Greeks Gods Figures Artwork by Ilona Freiburg

To Sam,
Whose love of Percy Jackson
is great training for New Testament Studies

Table of Contents

Contributors	ix
Acknowledgements	xi
Abbreviations	xiii
SBL Panel Papers on *The Gospels and Homer* and *Luke and Vergil*	1
Mainstreaming Mimesis Criticism	3
Mark G. Bilby	
Even Good Homer Nods	17
Michael Kochenash	
Mark and Homer	25
Kay Higuera Smith	
SBL Panel Papers on *The Dionysian Gospel*	35
Neos Dionysos in Textual and Cultural Mimesis	37
Richard C. Miller	
John's Politics of Imitation	43
Chan Sok Park	
The First Dionysian Gospel Imitational and Redactional Layers in Luke and John	49
Mark G. Bilby	
Mimesis in Practice	69
Discovering Old Imitations Anew	
Scriptural Revision in Mark's Gospel and Philostratus's Life of Apollonius	71
Austin Busch	

Acts 2 as an Intertextual Map **Moving from Dionysian to** **Platonic Identity** *Ilseo Park*	113
The Scandal of Gentile Inclusion **Reading Acts 17 with Euripides'** *Bacchae* *Michael Kochenash*	125
Objections, Reflections, and **Anticipations** *Dennis R. MacDonald*	145
Bibliography	157
Indices	173

Contributors

Mark G. Bilby, PhD (University of Virginia), is Senior Assistant Librarian of Scholarly Communications and Lecturer in Religious Studies at California State University, Fullerton, and the author of *As the Bandit Will I Confess You: Luke 23, 39–43 in Early Christian Interpretation* (University of Strasbourg / Brepols).

Austin Busch, PhD (Indiana University), is Associate Professor of English at the State University of New York, Brockport, and co-editor of the Norton Critical Edition of *The English Bible, King James Version*.

Margaret Froelich, PhD candidate (Claremont School of Theology), is co-editor of the Festschrift for Dennis MacDonald entitled *Christian Origins and the New Testament in the Greco-Roman Context*.

Michael Kochenash, PhD (Claremont School of Theology), is the author of articles in the *Journal of Biblical Literature*, *New Testament Studies*, the *Catholic Biblical Quarterly*, and *Novum Testamentum* and co-editor of *Christian Origins and the New Testament in the Greco-Roman Context*.

Dennis R. MacDonald, PhD (Harvard University), is Research Professor of New Testament at Claremont School of Theology and author of several groundbreaking books on the New Testament and mimesis criticism.

Richard C. Miller, PhD (Claremont Graduate University), is the author of *Resurrection and Reception in Early Christianity* (Routledge) and an article in the *Journal of Biblical Literature*.

Chan Sok Park, ThD (Harvard Divinity School), is Instructor in Religious Studies at the College of Wooster.

Ilseo Park, PhD candidate (Claremont School of Theology), is Adjunct Faculty in New Testament at Presbyterian Theological Seminary in America and co-editor of a Festschrift for Dennis MacDonald entitled *Christian Origins and the New Testament in the Greco-Roman Context*.

Kay Higuera Smith, PhD (Claremont Graduate University), is Professor in the Department of Biblical and Religious Studies at Azusa Pacific University and editor of *Evangelical Postcolonial Conversations: Global Awakenings in Theology and Praxis* (InterVarsity Press).

Acknowledgements

Dennis R. MacDonald has mentored and befriended many throughout his astute academic career, and the contributors to this book are proud to be in this good company. We would like to thank the General Editor of Claremont Press and Dean of the Library at Claremont School of Theology, Thomas E. Phillips, for encouraging this book from the very beginning and for supporting several of us in our academic research and writing. Azusa Pacific University and Yonsei University extended warm hospitality as hosts of the two Society of Biblical Literature conferences out of which the first two parts of this book arose.

Abbreviations

AB	Anchor Bible
AJP	*American Journal of Philology*
BibInt	Biblical Interpretation Series
BTS	Biblical Tools and Studies
BZNW	Beihefte zur Zeitschrift für die neutestamentliche Wissenschaft
CBR	*Currents in Biblical Research*
CSNTCO	Claremont Studies in New Testament & Christian Origins
ECC	Eerdmans Critical Commentary
ECHC	Early Christianity in Its Hellenistic Context
EH	Europäische Hochschulschriften
ETL	*Ephemerides Theologicae Lovanienses*
GR	*Greece & Rome*
GRBS	*Greek, Roman, and Byzantine Studies*
HTR	*Harvard Theological Review*
IBS	*Irish Biblical Studies*
ICC	International Critical Commentary
JBL	*Journal of Biblical Literature*
JECS	*Journal of Early Christian Studies*
JHC	*Journal of Higher Criticism*
JHS	*Journal of Hellenic Studies*
JSNT	*Journal for the Study of the New Testament*
JSNTSup	Journal for the Study of the New Testament Supplement Series
JSRC	Jerusalem Studies in Religion and Culture
JTS	*Journal of Theological Studies*
LCL	Loeb Classical Library
LNTS	Library of New Testament Studies
Mnemosyne	*Mnemosyne: A Journal of Classical Studies*
MTSR	*Method & Theory in the Study of Religion*

NICNT	New International Commentary on the New Testament
NovT	*Novum Testamentum*
NovTSup	Supplements to Novum Testamentum
*NPNF*²	*Nicene and Post-Nicene Fathers*, Series 2
NTGL	New Testament and Greek Literature
NTL	New Testament Library
NTS	*New Testament Studies*
NTTSD	New Testament Tools, Studies and Documents
OCT	Oxford Classical Texts/Scriptorum classicorum bibliotheca oxoniensis
OPIAC	Occasional Papers of the Institute for Antiquity and Christianity
Paideia	Paideia: Commentaries on the New Testament
Phil	*Philologus*
PRSt	*Perspectives in Religious Studies*
STAC	Studien und Texte zu Antike Christentum
TANZ	Texte und Arbeiten zum neutestamentlichen Zeitalter
TENTS	Texts and Editions for New Testament Study
TZ	*Theologische Zeitschrift*
WGRW	Writings from the Greco-Roman World
WUNT	Wissenschaftliche Untersuchungen zum Neuen Testament
ZAC	*Zeitschrift für Antikes Christentum/Journal of Ancient Christianity*
ZNW	*Zeitschrift für die neutestamentliche Wissenschaft*

SBL Panel Papers on Mark and Homer and Luke-Acts and Vergil

Mainstreaming Mimesis Criticism
Mark G. Bilby

In the last three years (2015–2017), Dennis MacDonald has published three seminal books reflecting a lifetime of scholarship.[1] Each book of this trilogy makes a magisterial contribution to scholarship and exemplifies the value of mimesis criticism as a methodology for Biblical studies. MacDonald shows beyond any reasonable doubt that (1) Mark imitates Homer's *Iliad* and *Odyssey*; that (2) Luke expands Mark's Homeric parallels to include Euripides' *Bacchae,* Plato's *Republic, Apology,* and *Phaedo,* and Vergil's *Aeneid* as well; and that (3) John models Jesus after Dionysus and the Pentheus of the *Bacchae* of Euripides. If these seminal texts are taken seriously—as they must be—they will radically transform New Testament studies as a community, discipline, discourse, and body of literature.

This chapter and those that follow have taken these books seriously, and quickly at that. The original version of this chapter and the next two were presented at the Society of Biblical Literature Pacific Coast Region meeting at Azusa Pacific University in Azusa, California, on March 9, 2015. These papers responded to review copies MacDonald graciously provided of his freshly published 2015 volumes entitled *The Gospel and Homer: Imitations of Greek Epic in Mark and Luke-Acts* and *Luke and Vergil: Imitations of Classical Greek*

---

[1] Dennis R. MacDonald, *The Gospels and Homer: Imitations of Greek Epic in Mark and Luke-Acts* (NTGL 1; Lanham, MD: Rowman & Littlefield, 2015); Dennis R. MacDonald, *Luke and Vergil: Imitations of Classical Greek Literature* (NTGL 2; Lanham, MD: Rowman & Littlefield, 2015); and Dennis R. MacDonald, *The Dionysian Gospel: The Fourth Gospel and Euripides* (Minneapolis: Fortress, 2017).

Literature. The next three papers were originally presented at the International Society of Biblical Literature meeting at Yonsei University in Seoul, South Korea, on July 4, 2016. For this session, MacDonald graciously provided pre-published versions of his forthcoming 2017 volume *The Dionysian Gospel: The Fourth Gospel and Euripides*. Both panels carried a range of voices, yet all resounded in their appreciation of the heroic academic feat that MacDonald accomplished in this trilogy.

All six of these chapters look with critical appreciation on MacDonald's recent work, support mimesis criticism becoming a vital and standard methodology within New Testament studies, and sometimes propose new directions of mimetic inquiry. In his chapter, "Even Good Homer Nods," Michael Kochenash describes numerous strengths of mimesis as a methodology, contemplates a more agnostic accounting of sources for Jesus traditions than in MacDonald's mythopoesis, and outlines future directions for scholarship in terms of making LXX-epic pairings and addressing how classical emulations eludicate authorial motivations. In "Mark and Homer," Kay Higuera Smith challenges MacDonald's claim that Mark directly depended on Homer, something Smith sees as unlikely because of Mark's lack of a classical education, his marginal (subaltern) socioeconomic status, and his limited sociolinguistic competence. Smith ultimately acknowledges the tremendous value of mimesis criticism, but only in terms of indirect oral and cultural influence. In "Neos Dionysos in Textual and Cultural Mimesis," Richard C. Miller esteems MacDonald's recent contributions while lamenting the general ignorance of classical epic within Biblical scholarship and the tendency to dismiss major contributions by means of minor objections. Miller appreciates the way MacDonald has broadened mimesis from a methodology focused on texts to one illuminating standard cultural models, and he adeptly frames the Dionysian imitations with the first edition of the Gospel of John as "asceticized Bacchanalia." In "John's Politics of Imitation," Chan Sok Park situates MacDonald's work on John and Euripides within two significant areas of Johannine scholarship: its indebtedness to Greek drama and its compositional history. He rhetorically presses on the issue of the "politics of imitation," wondering whether the Johannine community as well as the Luke-Acts community arose out of Dionysian cults or instead in competition with them. He also wonders what mimesis criticism would say about the absence of the Lord's Supper in John and what implicit and explicit claims about the Johannine community that MacDonald is making. In "The First Dionysian Gospel: Imitational and Redactional Layers in Luke and John," Mark G. Bilby describes how his doubts about mimesis were overcome by the numerous, dense parallels between Euripides' *Bacchae* and John. His primary objection is that MacDonald presumes the dependence of John (in three versions) on Luke-Acts (in a single version). Bilby instead provides an alternative, groundbreaking reconstruction of the Synoptic Problem. He shows that the rise of a Marcionite (or proto-Marcionite) exclusive Paulinism *and* Pliny the Younger's anti-Bacchanalian trials of Christians are historical, redactional-mimetic pivot points between the first and second editions of both John and Luke. Dionysian appropriations in the first editions of John and Luke are corrected and outdone by Socratic (counter-Dionysian) appropriations and the rehabilitation of Peter in the second editions of John and Luke.

The final three chapters focus on close mimetic analysis of specific passages in the Gospels and Acts, while also tracing out broader literary and theological implications for the New Testament, early Christianity, and the reception of epic literature in late antiquity. "Scriptural Revision in Mark's Gospel and Philostratus's *Life of Apollonius*," by Austin Busch, is a major contribution to the study of the Gospel of Mark. By means of a riveting, parallel tour of the reception of Homeric cyclops lore in these two texts, Busch recasts Mark's entire narrative as a retelling of the anthropophagic redemption myths of Odysseus-Polyphemus and Zeus-Chronos, all the while reframing mimesis criticism within the broader framework of the reception of classical epic. Ilseo Park offers a glimpse of his doctoral dissertation under MacDonald in his "Acts 2 as an Intertextual Map: Moving from Dionysian to Platonic Identity," showing how the Pentecost narrative establishes the mimetic program for the entire narrative of Acts, evoking yet displacing Dionysian motifs with Socratic ones. Finally, in "The Scandal of Gentile Inclusion: Reading Acts 17 with Euripides' *Bacchae*." Michael Kochenash confirms MacDonald's claim of the clear imitation of Jason the Argonaut in Acts 17:5b-9, yet Kochenash goes further to explain how this imitation functions to provide reassurance that Paul was no political threat. He also finds an additional imitation not previously mentioned by MacDonald: that Acts 17:1-5a evokes the *Bacchae* in its description of a religious movement arriving across the Aegean, its remarkable success among prominent women, and the anxious response of those in authority. He finally describes the significance of this imitation as a recasting of Gentile inclusion in Jewish communities as on par with Dionysian sexual scandal and as an assurance that Christians will in Dionysian fashion overcome opposition from the Pentheus-like Jewish leaders. Building on MacDonald's work while expanding it, these three chapters will make their own impact on scholarship and transform the way that numerous passages in the Gospels and Acts are understood. We will not summarize the conclusion here, except to say that Dennis MacDonald, whose words have inspired this volume, is accorded the honor of having the last word.

Mimetic Shame and Honor in New Testament Scholarship

In keeping with antiquity's penchant for honor and shame, celebration and lament, let us pause to ponder how strange this volume is within the broader context of New Testament scholarship. No tragic inventory is needed, for we all know that mimesis criticism as a methodology is almost entirely absent from popular introductions to the New Testament, as well as from primers and surveys of critical methodologies for the study of the New Testament. The same can be said for Biblical studies curricula, syllabi, reading lists, lectures, etc., whether at research universities or liberal arts colleges with religious affiliations. Throughout the educational enterprise, mimesis criticism is seldom mentioned, and when it is, it is too often stereotyped and dismissed out of hand. Academic societies such as SBL lack sufficient program units and sessions devoted to mimesis criticism, and mimesis criticism is not well-represented in sessions devoted to source, redaction, rhetorical, and literary criticism, where there should be natural affinities and collaborations. Most troubling of all is that graduate programs in New Testament studies so seldom require any kind of serious training in, or exposure to, the most commonly read, widely cited, and publicly performed narratives of that day. While ostensibly prioritizing Christianity's Jewish roots, New Testament studies so often privilege an anachronistically canonical Judaism that is ethnically monolithic, textually isolated, and linguistically ghettoized, instead of accounting for the diverse, cosmopolitan, and often quite Hellenized-Romanized kinds of Judaism practiced around and within the broader social and literary contexts of the New Testament.

This tragedy need not continue, and it must not. The publication of MacDonald's trilogy should settle the case once and for all that mimesis criticism is a serious, necessary, and valuable approach to the study of the New Testament. From here forward, any New Testament introduction or methodological primer that does not include and deploy mimesis criticism should be considered outdated and incomplete. From here forward, any curriculum or class pertaining to the New Testament that does not address and teach mimesis criticism should be considered outdated and incomplete. From here forward, any SBL gathering that lacks numerous sessions and vigorous discussions about mimetic critical readings should be considered outdated and incomplete. From here forward, any graduate program in New Testament studies that lacks in-depth exploration of the Greek and Latin classics should be considered outdated and incomplete. From here forward, any treatment of the Jewish roots of Christianity that does not account for the influence of the Greek and Latin classics on the kinds of Judaism practiced around and within the New Testament should be considered outdated and incomplete.

From One Man to a Methodological Movement

While MacDonald's work is seminal, it cannot stand on its own. One person may pioneer a movement, but he cannot make it. As mimesis criticism becomes more mainstream and widespread, it must become more nuanced, more diverse, and yes, more contentious, too. MacDonald's pioneering effort to explore all the potential classical antetexts behind Mark, Luke-Acts, and John is invaluable. Yet, as primarily the work of one person rather than a community or school, it is inevitably going to be idiosyncratic at points. These idiosyncrasies can unjustly lead to the whole of the work falling victim to ignorant caricature. For example, naysayers may deride MacDonald as engaged in just another form of the kind of parallelomania that Samuel Sandmel eschewed or seek to invalidate the whole of the work by pointing out weaknesses in a few parts.[2]

Even MacDonald's most avid supporters take issue with some of his mimetic readings, which is only natural.

---

[2] See Samuel Sandmel, "Parallelomania," *JBL* 81.1 (1962): 1–13.

Indeed, as the lead editor of this highly appreciative volume about MacDonald's works, I myself find some adduced parallels as not rising to the level of clear imitation/mimesis. Along with many readers of MacDonald's work, I find various New Testament texts and motifs to be better elucidated with reference to specific Jewish rather than Greco-Roman sources, that is, to the Septuagint more than Homer, Euripides, or Vergil.[3] That said, I must admit that literary allusions need not be mutually exclusive. Indeed, hybridity is a hallmark of thoughtful literature.

Yet it is not merely specific parallels where I find myself doubting. Sometimes these doubts run along patterns of argumentation. Can I trust an adduced parallel if the titles given to the passages are paraphrases made by the person proposing the parallel? Do the translations overly privilege

---

[3] With regard to *The Gospels and Homer*, for example, I have doubts about the strength of the parallel adduced regarding the glow emanating from Achilles in the *Iliad* and Stephen in Acts. See MacDonald, *Gospels and Homer*, 77–79. A Jewish/Septuagintal antetext (Moses's glowing face in Exod 34:29–35) seems more likely than a Homeric one. By way of context, MacDonald's earliest publication on mimesis criticism (*Christianizing Homer: The Odyssey, Plato, and the Acts of Andrew* [Oxford: Oxford University Press, 1994]) was preceded by Thomas L. Brodie's work exploring Luke's imitations of Septuagintal narratives. See especially Thomas L. Brodie, "The Accusing and Stoning of Naboth (1 Kgs 21:8–13) as One Component of the Stephen Text (Acts 6:9–14; 7:58a)," *CBQ* 45.3 (1983): 417–32; Thomas L. Brodie, "Luke-Acts as an Imitation and Emulation of the Elijah-Elisha Narrative," *New Views on Luke and Acts* (ed. Earl Richard; Wilmington: Glazier, 1983), 78–85; Thomas L. Brodie, "Greco-Roman Imitation of Texts as a Partial Guide to Luke's Use of Sources," *Luke-Acts: New Perspectives from the Society of Biblical Literature Seminar* (ed. Charles H. Talbert; New York: Crossroad, 1984), 17–46; Thomas L. Brodie, "Towards Unraveling Luke's Use of the Old Testament: Luke 7.11–17 as an *Imitatio* of 1 Kings 17.17–24," *NTS* 32.2 (1986): 247–67; and Thomas L. Brodie, "Not Q but Elijah: The Saving of the Centurion's Slave (Luke 7:1–10) as an Internalization of the Saving of the Widow and Her Child," *IBS* 14.2 (1992): 54–71.

the adduced parallels, and would other attempts at translation make certain parallels less plausible? Can the centuries-long gap between Homeric dialects and Koine Greek words be so easily surmounted? Are common narrative verbs (e.g., of seeing or saying) in parallel texts significant enough to note as evidence?

As a relatively new yet highly engaged reader of MacDonald's works, I certainly have my fair share of doubts. But I must also concede that I am not as capable of catching imitations as MacDonald is or others are. My doctoral studies did include extensive training in classical languages and literature. Yet I recognize that my cultural familiarity with Homer, Euripides, and Vergil pales in comparison to that of MacDonald and many classicists, and likely even pales in comparison to the rudimentary education and cultural experience shared among the authors and editors of the books that became the New Testament. Thus, my own sophomoric inability to detect literary clues and dramatic cues does not invalidate their existence. My doubts do not disprove. Rather, they invite me to immerse myself more deeply in the classics so that I might become capable of seeing the emulations and allusions that the New Testament authors/editors may well have seen and made.

All of this explains why mimesis criticism must move beyond one person and become a widely practiced methodology and discourse. Editorial committees and communities of scholars routinely collaborate to decide on matters of textual criticism and historical criticism. Why not for mimesis criticism also? It would be instructive to have groups or sessions, whether in-person or online, debate and even vote on whether a given mimetic parallel is reasonable or not. Perhaps they will together rank each as to whether it is (1) certain, (2) likely, (3) unlikely, or (4) impossible. Perhaps they will attempt to delineate modes of intertextuality, as to whether a given parallel may best be described as a quotation, emulation, allusion, or otherwise a loose similarity, such as a general cultural phrase, *topos*, or custom. Such nuances and distinctions are present (mostly implicitly) across MacDonald's analysis and discussion. This is no criticism, for his goal was not to act in place of a community of discourse, but rather to launch a serious discursive endeavor and give it a large body of evidence to navigate and map more carefully. As MacDonald himself told me, he has attempted in these volumes to throw every possible parallel against the barn, and he looks forward to seeing what sticks to the scholarly community. Whatever the categories, the nuances, the groups, and the fora, what is most important is that there be a shared, substantive, and consequential discussion among scholars that takes seriously these classical parallels, as well as those discovered or proposed by others.

Mimesis and Early Christian History

For mimesis to get a fair hearing, we also must address faith-based approaches to the New Testament and how mimesis criticism relates to them. Many religiously minded scholars may find mimesis criticism unpalatable as just another example of the influence of secularism, neo-paganism, or even atheism. Even so, as with other methodologies in Biblical studies (e.g., source, form, and redaction criticism), mimesis criticism need not be construed as anti-Christian or anti-theological *per se*. It can easily be deployed in ways that comport with, rather than undermine, traditional theological and literary interpretations of the Gospels.

It is true that MacDonald's default historical explanation of literary parallels is *mythopoesis*, that is, fabrication of characters and stories to recall and rival classical models. But this default for MacDonald does not have to obtain for all mimesis critics. Indeed, some of the contributors to this book personally embrace an Evangelical and/or Orthodox Christian identity and confession. Their participation itself is proof that, to his friends, students, and colleagues—whether in the church, the academy, or both—MacDonald has a well-earned reputation as someone who is hospitable to and inclusive of persons of Christian faith and someone whose methodology can be practiced by practicing Christians. For some of these contributors, like many of the scholars reading this book, Mary Magdalene, Mary the mother of Jesus, Judas Iscariot, Joseph of Arimathea, Stephen, and others should be considered historical persons, and their actions as described in the New Testament ought to be considered as having some basis in history. Yet these convictions regarding historicity are not mutually exclusive with the conclusion that their stories and perhaps even their names took on legendary overtones in their tellings and retellings. *Mythopoesis* need not merely fabricate out of whole cloth; it can also embroider upon an underlying tapestry.[4]

I wonder if MacDonald himself would agree with this.[5] For example, would he grant that Paul was a historical figure, even as the historical Paul undergoes legendary transformations between his authentic and inauthentic letters, and between his authentic letters and Acts? If so, why should Paul be considered historical but not many of the players in the Gospels? Is it because he wrote? To turn a phrase, is it the case for MacDonald's mythopoetic Cartesianism that *scribo ergo sum*? If authorship is not the defining criterion of historical existence, then, for scholars more generally, Paul could very well be considered a paradigm for mimesis-critical readings of major players in the Gospels and Acts, rather than an exception to them.

---

[4] See also Michael Kochenash, "Even Good Homer Nods," *infra* and Richard C. Miller, "Neos Dionysos in Textual and Cultural Mimesis," *infra*.

[5] See Dennis R. MacDonald, "Conclusion: Objections, Reflections, and Anticipations," *infra*.

Additionally, scholars may find in the Gospels historical characters who took on dramatic roles in actual life and not merely in later literature. Joseph of Arimathea, for example, need not be a complete fabrication for him to play the part of noble Priam begging the body of his son, or the part of righteous Tobit burying the bodies of the dead. To paraphrase Shakespeare in *As You Like It* (II.vii), life itself is a drama, and we humans play our parts. Art imitates art, true, yet art imitates life, and life art.

Mimesis and Early Christian Theology

Besides historicity, theology also factors into the capacity of mimesis criticism to gain broader traction among faith-conscious scholars. Time and again, what struck me in MacDonald's works were the ways in which mimesis-critical readings underscored a *high* Christology. The Jesuses of Mark, Luke, and John not only surpassingly emulate the roles and feats of epic heroes, but also those of epic deities. One might see in many mimesis critical readings so many opportunities for theologians and preachers to proclaim a Christ that does not merely recall but completely surpasses all other models and objects of devotion. Church historians and historical theologians might likewise be invited to explore just how pivotal these *surpassing imitations* were to the ascendancy of a high Christology in early Christianity. Yes, pre-Hellenistic Jewish texts and traditions played their roles, as did Jewish- and early Christian-Platonic ones. But the high Christology of the Gospels may owe as much if not more to the Greco-Roman mimesis practiced by Mark, Luke, and John than to Jewish monotheistic, messianic, wisdom, and word traditions, which were themselves profoundly transformed and shaped by Jewish appropriations of Hellenistic philosophy. Early Christology took flight not only on the wings of Hellenistic philosophy but also those of Greek epic.

Let us specifically address scholars who have dismissed MacDonald's work from the vantage of the study of the church fathers (patristics) or early Christianity more broadly conceived. One of MacDonald's criteria to demonstrate intertextuality—"ancient and Byzantine recognitions"—is not only valuable here, but also indicative of a massive area for future research, writing, discussion, and debate.[6] For the sake of greater terminological precision and academic breadth (to include receptions in Latin, Syriac, Coptic, etc.), I would term this criterion "overlapping afterlives" or "overlapping reception histories."

MacDonald does an admirable job of showing how the classics and the Gospels are clearly intertwined in the Acts of Andrew and the Homeric Centos.[7] But there are many rich studies yet to be done on the overlapping reception histories to be found among Christian apologists (especially Justin Martyr, Clement of Alexandria, Origen of Alexandria, and even Augustine), Christian historians (especially Lactantius and Eusebius), early Christian epic poets (especially Juvencus and Prudentius), and the early critics of Christianity (especially Celsus, Porphyry, and Julian). Christian art is yet another broad avenue of inquiry in this regard. What may look like syncretism in the anachronistic eyes of an uninformed or religiously zealous post-classicism may actually be a kind of cultural and religious hybridity of the very sort mimesis criticism takes as commonplace.

While explicit, textual evidence of overlapping reception histories should be front and center, we should also keep in mind how the Gospel emulations of classical texts were so obvious as to be assumed. Where some scholars see minimal explicit awareness among early Christians of these overlaps, with just a slight shift of perspective one can see

---

[6] See, e.g., MacDonald, *Gospels and Homer*, 6–7.
[7] See MacDonald, *Gospels and Homer*, 327–86.

them implicitly present everywhere precisely because they were taken for granted as part of the Hellenistic air that everyone in Roman antiquity breathed. As mentioned, the Gospel emulations of Homer, Euripides, and Vergil played a major role in the ascendancy of a high Christology. But these emulations also continued underwriting high Christologies for centuries thereafter in their ongoing performances. Indeed, the Christological controversies of ancient Christianity can easily be read as the profoundly difficult effort to come to terms with the implications of the appropriation of classical models in the Gospels. How to reconcile Jewish monotheism with the epic depictions of Jesus—this lies at the heart of early Christian theological debates and liturgies. These debates also repeatedly evince a lively tension between competing appropriations of Greek epic and Greek philosophy. As readers will see later, this tension stood at the core of the emergence of proto-Orthodox/Catholic Christianity and was already very much in evidence in Acts and the later redactional layers of the Gospel of John and Gospel of Luke.[8] Even outside of Christian circles, we find that the primary objections lodged by rabbinic Judaism and Islam against Jesus's deification and Trinitarian theology demonstrate an incisive awareness of the patently obvious connections between classical stories and early Christian claims, and an informed objection to Christian theology being a legitimate appropriation of Jewish monotheism and Greek philosophy.

For those who are not blinded by prejudicial *a priori* assumptions of Christian uniqueness, early Christian

---

[8] Regarding the programmatic and repeated epic (Dionysian) and philosophical (Socratic) tensions in Acts, see Ilseo Park, "Acts 2 as an Intertextual Map: Moving from Dionysian to Platonic Identity," *infra*. Regarding those same tensions evidenced in the compositional-redactional histories of John and Luke, see Mark G. Bilby, "The First Dionysian Gospel: Imitational and Redactional Layers in Luke and John," *infra*.

historical theology is clearly both an expansion of and defense against its own *surpassing imitations* of Greek epic and Greek philosophy. Thus mimesis is no mere appendage to Christianity and its related academic disciplines. Because classical imitation is at the heart of the New Testament, it is also at the heart of patristics, historical theology, church history, art history, and even interreligious studies.

Even Good Homer Nods
Michael Kochenash

"Quandoque bonus dormitat Homerus"

The writings of Euripides, Plato, Xenophon, and, above all, Homer were so influential within the Roman Mediterranean world that even a simple comparison of the Gospel narratives and Acts with them ought to be recognized as inherently valuable.[1] Yet, in *The Gospels and Homer* and *Luke and Vergil*, Dennis MacDonald adeptly demonstrates that close comparisons reveal parallels that are so frequent and distinctive that it is most credible to posit an intertextual relationship.[2] These two books contribute to a growing trend among readers of the Gospels and Acts wherein critics read these narratives within the context of ancient literary compositional practices instead of viewing them as tralatitious patchworks.[3] The title of this chapter is taken from a Latin

---

[1] This is particularly true given the prominence of these writers in Greek literate education.

[2] Dennis R. MacDonald, *The Gospels and Homer: Imitations of Greek Epic in Mark and Luke-Acts* (NTGL 1; Lanham, MD: Rowman & Littlefield, 2015) and Dennis R. MacDonald, *Luke and Vergil: Imitations of Classical Greek Literature* (NTGL 2; Lanham, MD: Rowman & Littlefield, 2015).

[3] See, e.g., Burton L. Mack and Vernon K. Robbins, *Patterns of Persuasion in the Gospels* (Sonoma, CA: Polebridge, 1989); Vernon K. Robbins, "Writing as a Rhetorical Act in Plutarch and the Gospels," *Persuasive Artistry: Studies in New Testament Rhetoric in Honor of George A. Kennedy* (ed. Duane F. Watson; JSNTSup 50; Sheffield: JSOT, 1991), 157–86; Todd Penner, "Reconfiguring the Rhetorical Study of Acts: Reflections on the Method in and Learning of a Progymnastic Poetics," *PRSt* 30.3 (2003): 425–39; Timothy A. Brookins, "Luke's Use of Mark as παράφρασις: Its Effects on Characterization in the 'Healing of Blind Bartimaeus' Pericope (Mark 10.46–52/Luke 18.35–43)," *JSNT* 34.1 (2011): 70–89; *Luke's Literary*

phrase originating with Horace (*"quandoque bonus dormitat Homerus"* [*Ars* 359]). The idiom suggests that even the greatest thinkers are liable to the occasional solecism, but these imperfections do not diminish the significance of their work.

Reading the New Testament as Ancient Mediterranean Literature

MacDonald's *The Gospels and Homer* and *Luke and Vergil* have many merits; I foreground here five of their strengths. (1) MacDonald works inductively, drawing conclusions on the basis of a close reading of the Biblical texts and potential models, not on the basis of assumptions about the Biblical authors' levels of education.[4] (2) MacDonald makes sense of

---

Creativity (ed. Mogens Müller and Jesper Tang Nielsen. LNTS 550; London: Bloomsbury T&T Clark, 2016). See also Dennis R. MacDonald, *Does the New Testament Imitate Homer? Four Cases from the Acts of the Apostles* (New Haven: Yale University Press, 2003), 1–15.

[4] To be clear, MacDonald draws conclusions specifically about Mark's and Luke's familiarity with classical Greek texts on the basis of close comparisons. A Biblical author's familiarity with classical Greek texts is not necessarily indicative of the level of education attained by that author (i.e., primary, secondary, or tertiary). If the most credible conclusion based on a close comparison is that a Biblical author imitated a classical Greek text, then it is sensible to conclude that this Biblical author possessed the competence to do so — whatever the author's level of education. Indeed, some progymnastic strategies may have been incorporated at earlier stages of literate education than has been assumed, and mimetic strategies could be observed and acquired outside the classroom — in theaters, for example. On progymnastic exercises in early stages of literate education, see Sean A. Adams, "Luke and *Progymnasmata*: Rhetorical Handbooks, Rhetorical Sophistication and Genre Selection," *Ancient Education and Early Christianity* (ed. Matthew Ryan Hauge and Andrew W. Pitts; LNTS 533; London: Bloomsbury T&T Clark, 2016), 137–54. Some scholars offer an alternative inductive analysis on the basis of Mark's poor grammar. They argue, for example, that because Mark exhibits a poor grasp of grammar, it is unlikely that Mark achieved a high level of literate education, and so it is unlikely that Mark imitated Homer in the way MacDonald describes. See, e.g., Kay Higuera Smith, "Mark and

Mark and Luke-Acts as products of literate education during the imperial period. He moves beyond twentieth-century models for the composition of these narratives (specifically source and form criticism) and analyzes them within their ancient Mediterranean compositional context.[5] (3) MacDonald identifies a compelling strategy for creating meaning in antiquity, arguing that Mark and Luke communicate meaning about Jesus, Peter, Paul, and the kingdom of God by reference to familiar narratives and characters: Hector, Achilles, Odysseus, and Telemachus (and, in Luke-Acts, Dionysus, Pentheus, and Socrates).

(4) Many of MacDonald's readings account for what appear to be non sequiturs in the Biblical narratives.[6] It would be tedious to enumerate examples, so I will instead describe how MacDonald's reading of Luke-Acts as a Christian *Iliad-Odyssey* may shed light on a long-standing interpretive issue, a non sequitur of sorts: why is an account of Paul's death absent from Acts?[7] Luke hints at Paul's death (e.g., Acts 20:25) but omits its narration, a situation that is all the more

---

Homer," *infra*. Such scholars may be correct with respect to Mark's level of education, but their explanations of Markan parallels with Homer are less credible than MacDonald's. See also Dennis R. MacDonald, "Conclusion: Objections, Reflections, and Anticipations," *infra*.

[5] Of course, MacDonald does not reject source criticism by any means. See, e.g., Dennis R. MacDonald, *Two Shipwrecked Gospels: The* Logoi *of Jesus and Papias's* Exposition of Logia about the Lord (ECL 8; Atlanta: Society of Biblical Literature, 2012) and Dennis R. MacDonald, *The Dionysian Gospel: The Fourth Gospel and Euripides* (Minneapolis: Fortress, 2017).

[6] For example, MacDonald reads Mark 4:35-41 as imitating Homer, *Od.* 10.1-77, which accounts for Mark's perplexing notice that "other boats were with him" (Mark 4:36), because twelve ships accompanied Odysseus in the Homeric model. See MacDonald, *Gospels and Homer*, 204-08.

[7] For Luke-Acts as a Christian *Iliad-Odyssey*—in response to Virgil's *Odyssey-Iliad*—see MacDonald, *Luke and Vergil*, 1-5.

confounding in light of the Socratic nature of Paul's trials throughout the final third of Acts.[8] Homer's Odysseus, however, does not die within the poem. If the book of Acts is read as a Christian *Odyssey*, then there is no cause to wonder why Luke omits Paul's death. MacDonald's work routinely explains this type of quandary.

(5) Finally, MacDonald's books are structured in a helpful way for readers who are not familiar with the Greco-Roman classics in question. Instead of following the narrative order of New Testament texts, these books follow the order of Homer's *Iliad* and *Odyssey* (in *The Gospels and Homer*) and Euripides' *Bacchae*, the Socratic dialogues of Plato and Xenophon, and Vergil's *Aeneid* (in *Luke and Vergil*). In this way, readers can improve their familiarity with these classics.

A Proposal for Improved Reception

I have one primary criticism, though it relates to what I simultaneously view as a strength. I have already noted that MacDonald helps modern interpreters read the New Testament narratives within the context of ancient literary composition—much like scholars who read the New Testament from the perspective of the *progymnasmata* or

---

[8] On the Socratic nature of Paul's trials, see Dennis R. MacDonald, "A Categorization of Antetextuality in the Gospels and Acts: A Case for Luke's Imitation of Plato and Xenophon to Depict Paul as a Christian Socrates," *The Intertextuality of the Epistles: Explorations of Theory and Practice* (ed. Thomas L. Brodie, Dennis R. MacDonald, and Stanley E. Porter; Sheffield: Sheffield Phoenix Press, 2006), 211–25; Rubén R. Dupertuis, "Bold Speech, Opposition, and Philosophical Imagery in Acts," *Engaging Early Christian History: Reading Acts in the Second Century* (ed. Rubén R. Dupertuis and Todd Penner; London: Routledge, 2014), 153–68; Ryan Carhart, "The Second Sophistic and the Cultural Idealization of Paul in Acts," *Engaging Early Christian History: Reading Acts in the Second Century* (ed. Rubén R. Dupertuis and Todd Penner; London: Routledge, 2014), 187–208; and MacDonald, *Luke and Vergil*, 90–96.

rhetorical handbooks.⁹ I find this paradigm shift helpful, but some readers will likely be turned off by MacDonald's assertion that Mark and Luke created narratives from scratch in order to imitate literary models. Instead, an agnostic approach might be more palatable for a broader reading public. Mark and Luke may have created narratives inspired by nothing more than their literary models on occasion. At other times, however, they may have been inspired to elaborate their compositions due to the similarities between traditions about Jesus, Peter, and Paul and certain exemplary literary models.

MacDonald recognizes this latter possibility only when he is aware of the source of a tradition, usually the lost Gospel (Q+) or something that informed Josephus.¹⁰ For instance, when discussing the beheading of John the Baptist in Mark 6, MacDonald recognizes that a tradition existed concerning this event.¹¹ Although he finds compelling parallels, suggesting imitation, between Mark and the story of Agamemnon's death in book 11 of the *Odyssey*—both are narrated as a flashback, and both involve marital infidelity, a threat to the continuation of the infidelity, a beheading of the threat, and a mealtime setting—he recognizes, by merit of Josephus's awareness that Herod Antipas executed John, that Mark did not invent all of the details in his account. I wonder whether an agnosticism about possible sources could have improved the chances of positive reception among moderate conservatives on the one hand and liberals approaching the

---

⁹ See n. 3 above.

¹⁰ On Q+, see MacDonald, *Two Shipwrecked Gospels*.

¹¹ MacDonald, *Gospels and Homer*, 239–43. Josephus discusses John's death in *A.J.* 18.116-119.

narratives from a twentieth-century form-critical framework on the other.[12]

Trajectories for Future Scholarship: Hybridity and Motivation

In many ways, these books represent the culmination of MacDonald's decades of work on Mark and Luke-Acts; readers have much for which to be grateful. The mark of truly great scholarship is that others can follow and create valuable work of their own, standing on the shoulders of that scholarship. I can imagine at least two trajectories for future studies based on MacDonald's germinal work may be particularly rewarding, guided by these two questions. (1) How can we understand the emergent significance of Luke-Acts and Mark when they blend different classical and Septuagintal literary models within their narratives, whether within a single episode, in contiguous episodes, or in episodes in disparate narrative locations? (2) Is there more that can be done to strengthen the credibility of the claim that Mark and Luke imitate certain literary models, particularly in terms of identifying possible (and credible) motivations, a major concern of ancient literary critics?

As for the first trajectory, one example can be observed in the book of Acts. In *Luke and Vergil,* MacDonald argues for a cluster of imitations of Euripides' *Bacchae,* a tragic play about Dionysus bringing his cult from Turkey to Greece, in the first sixteen chapters of Acts, followed by a cluster of imitations of Socrates in Acts 17-28.[13] Ilseo Park, in an informal conversation, has suggested that the emergent picture of Paul is interpretively meaningful: in the *Bacchae,* the hero kills his opponent; in Socratic narratives, the hero himself dies at the

---

[12] Mark G. Bilby, " Mainstreaming Mimesis Criticism," *supra,* offers similar critiques.

[13] MacDonald, *Luke and Vergil,* 121-23.

hands of his opponents.[14] Luke's motivation for generating this emergent mimetic characterization might have stemmed from what he knew to be the case: Rome executed Paul; Paul didn't kill Nero. On the other hand, he might have been trying to articulate Paul's identity in a culturally meaningful way by reference (and contrast) to these literary models: Paul was both similar to and different from both Dionysus and Socrates, and the comparison with Socrates gets the final word. The combinations available for exploration are numerous: for example, Paul (Acts 27) as a Jonah/Odysseus (from the *Odyssey*) figure, Peter (Acts 10-11) as a Jonah/Odysseus (from the *Iliad*) figure, and Jesus (Luke 22-23) as a Socrates/Hector figure.[15]

The second trajectory concerns motivation.[16] One example involves Mark's and Luke's imitations of Homer's *Iliad*. In the background of the *Iliad* is the eventual destruction of the city of Troy. Although Homer does not narrate its destruction or the Trojan horse that precedes it, the events of the *Iliad*'s narrative—particularly the climactic death of Hector—directly contribute to that end. Given that Mark and Luke wrote after the destruction of Jerusalem, their connection of Jesus's death to the city's fall supplies credible motivation for them to imitate the *Iliad*. The correspondence in details made Homer's poem an attractive and appropriate model for narrating broadly similar stories.

---

[14] See Ilseo Park, "Acts 2 as an Intertextual Map: Moving from Dionysian to Platonic Identity," *infra*.

[15] Another example of how blending models creates an emergent understanding of early Christianity can be seen in Michael Kochenash, "The Scandal of Gentile Inclusion: Reading Acts 17 with Euripides' *Bacchae*," *infra*, on Acts 17:1-10, where Paul's missionary activity and the responses to it are modeled on both Euripides' *Bacchae* and Pindar's *Pythian Ode* concerning Jason and the Golden Fleece.

[16] See also Chan Sok Park, "John's Politics of Imitation," *infra*.

I wonder whether attending to motivation might also address critics, such as Karl Olav Sandnes, in a way that has yet to be done. Sandnes suggests that there are no advertised macro-structural suggestions that Homer is being imitated in the New Testament narratives.[17] MacDonald addresses Sandnes's concern for the advertised nature of imitations but limits his response to micro-level advertisements.[18] Given that the purview of the literary project of Luke included both the life and death of Jesus and the activity of his disciples, from a macro-narrative perspective, I wonder whether it would have been more strange if Luke had *not* used Homer's epics as literary models.

In his two-volume work, the first of which climaxes with the noble death of Jesus and the second of which features the sea-voyaging movements of Paul, Luke surely had sufficient motivation to imitate both Homer's macro-structure and, consequently, smaller narrative episodes to reinforce the larger rhetorical goal. There are comparably compelling suggestions to be explored for Luke's motivation to imitate the *Bacchae*; Socratic literature; and Septuagintal narratives about Moses, Samuel, David, Elijah, Elisha, and Jonah, all of which would fortify MacDonald's arguments. Be that as it may, it is my opinion that these books are nothing less than a gift to the scholarly community. They deserve to be read, *and reread*, with care.

---

[17] Cf. Karl Olav Sandnes, *The Gospel "according to Homer and Virgil": Cento and Canon* (NovTSup 138; Leiden: Brill, 2011), 49–50.

[18] E.g., MacDonald, *Gospels and Homer*, 10–13. See also Dennis R. MacDonald, *My Turn: A Critique of Critics of "Mimesis Criticism"* (OPIAC 53; Claremont, CA: Institute for Antiquity and Christianity, 2009).

Mark and Homer
Kay Higuera Smith

In his books *The Gospels and Homer* and *Luke and Vergil*, Dennis MacDonald has offered a compelling and systematic taxonomy of the use of classical Greek literature—especially Homer and Vergil—in the Gospels.[1] I will limit my comments here to his discussion of the Gospel of Mark and its literary parallels with Homer. In *The Gospels and Homer*, MacDonald writes, "The Markan Evangelist apparently did not inherit most of his characters and episodes from antecedent traditions and texts; he created them by imitating classical Greek poetry, especially the Homeric epics, the *Odyssey* above all."[2] MacDonald supports his claims for Markan imitation, or mimesis, of Homer by referencing ancient models of classical literary education that especially privileged the works of Homer.[3]

He argues not for indirect, but direct, influence of Homer upon the Markan author (to whom I will refer in shorthand as Mark), rejecting Bruce Louden's theory of indirect influence in favor of a theory of direct influence.[4] "Gospel authors," he retorts, "directly imitated Homer."[5] They produced "direct, extensive, advertised, and

---

[1] Dennis R. MacDonald, *The Gospels and Homer: Imitations of Greek Epic in Mark and Luke-Acts* (NTGL 1; Lanham, MD: Rowman & Littlefield, 2015) and Dennis R. MacDonald, *Luke and Vergil: Imitations of Classical Greek Literature* (NTGL 2; Lanham, MD: Rowman & Littlefield, 2015).

[2] MacDonald, *Gospels and Homer*, 2.

[3] MacDonald, *Gospels and Homer*, 3.

[4] See Bruce Louden, *Homer's* Odyssey *and the Near East* (Cambridge: Cambridge University Press, 2011).

[5] MacDonald, *Gospels and Homer*, 5.

hermeneutically freighted imitations of earlier writings."[6] I will challenge MacDonald on this assertion and argue that indirect influence is a much more plausible contention. Neither the Markan author's socioeconomic nor sociolinguistic location make it likely that Mark could have had the education or the rhetorical training that would be required to argue with sufficient plausibility that he followed ancient models of Greek education by consistently and directly imitating Homer and other classical Greek sources.

Mark's Lack of a Classical Education

First, MacDonald argues that it is very plausible that Mark would have received a classical education.[7] He contends that Mark's Gospel fulfills the criteria characteristic of literary mimesis as carried out by classically educated Greek writers of the era. These criteria include "accessibility, analogy, density, order, distinctive trait[s], and interpretability."[8] In making this claim, however, MacDonald does not adequately address the counter-claim, which is that Mark's marginal socioeconomic status and his poor grammatical skills would have made a classical education unlikely. MacDonald dismisses this argument, citing David Rhoads and Donald Michie, who argue that Mark was a sophisticated literary composer.[9] To be sure, the Markan author may indeed have

---

[6] MacDonald, *Gospels and Homer*, 6.

[7] Contra Michael Kochenash, "Even Good Homer Nods," *supra*.

[8] MacDonald, *Gospels and Homer*, 6. MacDonald also supports his claim that the Gospel writers imitated Homer by citing examples of other Jewish authors in this era who were classically trained and who clearly alluded to or explicitly imitated Greek writers (*Gospels and Homer*, 7–8). These include Philo, Theodotus, Josephus, and the writer of the Sibylline Oracles.

[9] MacDonald, *Gospels and Homer*, 389 n. 25. See David Rhoads and Donald Michie, *Mark as Story: An Introduction to the Narrative of a Gospel* (Philadelphia: Fortress, 1982).

had a keen eye for narrative, as Rhoads and Michie demonstrate. The author effectively weaves together all of the key elements of narrative—character, setting, plot line, and stock rhetorical conventions.[10] However, to be able to tell a good story is a far cry from employing the skills mastered through formal study of the classical texts of Greek antiquity. In fact, the style of Mark's Greek—which is not part of the analysis of Rhoads and Michie's narrative criticism—as well as Mark's social status, cast doubt on the assertion that Mark could have been the kind of sophisticated literary composer that MacDonald depicts.

MacDonald is certainly aware of Mark's poor Greek. But, he argues, "One can no longer assume that Marcus was *rusticus*." He does concede, however, that "even *hoi polloi* soaked up narrative poetry." In making this claim about *hoi polloi*, MacDonald argues that "ancient Greeks were not exposed to Homer exclusively from texts."[11] Which is it then? When arguing against Bruce Louden's theory of indirect influence, MacDonald rejects indirect influence in favor of direct, but when acknowledging the evidence against Mark having had access to classical education, MacDonald seems to be making an argument *for* indirect influence. It is unclear how he reconciles these two arguments.

Mark's Marginal Socioeconomic Status

MacDonald too quickly dismisses the important objection to his thesis that Mark is unlikely to have had a classical education in light of his marginal social standing. In dismissing this objection, MacDonald contends that Mark "was a Christian elite," a social status that presumably would make this kind of education plausible.[12] However, in the late

---

[10] Rhoads and Michie, *Mark as Story*, xi.
[11] MacDonald, *Gospels and Homer*, 9.
[12] MacDonald, *Gospels and Homer*, 9.

first century CE, a Christian elite was far from a social elite. During this period, high Christian status did not necessarily translate into high social status vis-à-vis the larger Greco-Roman world. To demonstrate Mark's affinity with those of low social status, note that Mark's Gospel shows great sympathy toward those who occupied the social margins under the Roman imperial system.[13] Both Jesus's teachings within Mark and Mark's narrations about the groups of people who followed Jesus describe people without adequate food to eat, "the little ones [τῶν μικρῶν]" (9:42), most likely including day laborers, peasant subsistence farmers and fishermen, the sick and disabled, and slaves (Mark 1:16–20, 45; 4:1; 4:2–10, 26–32; 5:21; 6:3, 33–34, 53–56; 8:1–9; 9:14; 13:16, 34–36).[14]

Political and economic references in Mark's Gospel—all from the social margins—also point to Mark's marginal socioeconomic status. Themes that reoccur in Mark include taxation (2:15; 12:13–17), tenant farming and debt slavery (12:1–9), economic exploitation (10:17–23; 12:40–44), and greed

---

[13] C. I. David Joy, *Mark and Its Subalterns: A Hermeneutical Paradigm for a Postcolonial Context* (London: Equinox, 2008), 64–65. The characters that pepper Mark's narrative are lepers (Mark 1:40; 14:3), those who were demon possessed (1:23–26, 32–34, 39; 3:11–12, 15, 22; 5:1–20; 6:13; 7:25–30), and the dispossessed and disabled (2:1–12; 3:1–5, 10; 5:25–34; 7:32–35; 8:22–26; 9:15–27; 10:46–52). Mark's affinity for the people of Galilee (1:28; 3:7; 4:1; 5:21, 24), a region known for its hostility toward the Roman occupation, his animosity toward the Jewish leaders and collaborators of Rome, and his distinct neglect for the well-established urban centers in the Galilee in favor of the villages (6:6) all point to a status of social marginalization and resistance to the accepted status markers of the Roman occupation.

[14] Joy, *Mark and Its Subalterns*, 70. Cf. Richard A. Horsley and John S. Hanson, *Bandits, Prophets, and Messiahs: Popular Movements at the Time of Jesus* (Minneapolis: Winston, 1985), 256, who remind us that Mark depicts Jesus, ultimately, as having been crucified between two bandits, or social brigands (Mark 15:27).

(4:19; 7:22). These are not the concerns of social elites but of those who identify with the social margins. Mark rejects even such basic status identifiers as kinship (3:31), and he rejects the status claims of those who "like to walk around in their long robes and be greeted in the markets and to have the premier seats in the synagogues and at the banquets" (12:38–39). As David F. Watson notes of Mark's Jesus, "In the marketplace of elite ambition, Jesus's claims would seem utter nonsense."[15] Given the concentration of themes, characters, and terms that ascribe honor to people of low status and reserve scorn for those in the upper classes, a strong scholarly consensus locates Mark not as an elite but as a subaltern and thus unlikely to have had access to, or even to have desired, the classical education sought after by ancient Mediterranean elites.[16]

---

[15] David F. Watson, "The *Life of Aesop* and the Gospel of Mark: Two Ancient Approaches to Elite Values," *JBL* 129.4 (2010): 699–716, here 702. Horsley and Hanson have demonstrated the class conflict present in Mark as well (see Mark 11:27–33). See Richard A. Horsley, *Hearing the Whole Story: The Politics of Plot in Mark's Gospel* (Louisville: Westminster John Knox, 2001), 179. Note that Mark assigns high status to prophets such as John, who wears only camel's hair and a leather belt (1:6), to children (10:14–15), the one who has left all (10:29–30), the servant or the slave (10:42–45), and the poor (12:42).

[16] Among the many scholars arguing for Mark as subaltern and Galileans as social resisters are: Fernando Belo, *A Materialist Reading of the Gospel of Mark* (Maryknoll, NY: Orbis, 1975); Douglas Edwards, "The Socio-economic and Cultural Ethos of the Lower Galilee in the First Century: Implications "for Nascent Jesus Movement," *The Galilee in Late Antiquity* (ed. L. I. Levine; New York: Jewish Theological Seminary of America, 1992), 14–72; Sean Freyne, "The Galileans in the Light of Josephus' *Vita*," *NTS* 26.3 (1980): 397–413; Horsley and Hanson, *Bandits, Prophets, and Messiahs*; Richard L. Rohrbaugh, "The Social Location of the Markan Audience," *Interpretation* 47.4 (1993): 380–95; Gerd Theissen, *Social Reality and the Early Christians: Theology, Ethics and the World of the New Testament* (Edinburgh: T&T Clark, 1993); and Ben Witherington III, *The Gospel of Mark: A Socio-Rhetorical Commentary* (Grand Rapids: Eerdmans, 2001).

Mark's Limited Sociolinguistic Competence

Finally, of course, we have the well-known evidence of Mark's Greek syntax and structure, which also challenges MacDonald's claim that Mark likely received an elite education. In 2011, Albert Hogeterp performed a sociolinguistic analysis of Mark's Greek and reaffirmed the conclusions of Adolf Deissmann that Mark's Greek represents a sociolinguistic product of the lower classes of bilingual Greek/Aramaic speakers.[17] Watson adds that, for Greek literary elites, "the commonest offenses were 'barbarism' and 'solecism,' neither of which," adds Watson, "is uncommon in Mark."[18]

Examples of Mark's solecistic, or ungrammatical, Greek include indiscriminate interchanging of verb number and tenses, run-on sentences connected by what H. B. Swete calls "the simplest of Greek copulas,"[19] endless repetition of adverbs such as "immediately [εὐθὺς]", as well as clumsy, inelegant, and awkward transitions, narratives, and use of literary conventions.[20] In the face of these sociolinguistic

---

[17] Albert L. A. Hogeterp, "New Testament Greek as Popular Speech: Adolf Deissmann in Retrospect," *ZNW* 102.2 (2011): 178–200, here 179. On the same page, he adds that Greek such as Mark's represents a significantly different sociolinguistic world in terms of class, status, and education than, say, a second-century gymnasiarch studying rhetoric and peppering his writing with Atticisms. Henry Barclay Swete, *The Gospel according to St. Mark: The Greek Text with Introduction, Notes and Indices* (3rd ed.; Grand Rapids: Eerdmans, 1956), xlvii, also concluded that Mark "was a foreigner who spoke Greek with some freedom, but had not been accustomed to employ it for literary purposes."

[18] Watson, "*Life of Aesop*," 702.

[19] Swete, *Gospel*, xlvii–iii and John C. Meagher, *Clumsy Construction in Mark's Gospel: A Critique of Form- and Redaktionsgeschichte* (Toronto Studies in Theology 3; New York: Mellen, 1979), 70.

[20] Meagher, *Clumsy Construction*, 68; see also Joel Marcus, *Mark 1–16: A New Translation with Introduction and Commentary* (2 vols.; AB 27–27A;

analyses of Mark, it is difficult to sustain the argument that his writings reflect an elite classical education.

The claim, then, that Mark was a high-status individual who would have had access to classical Greek education is belied by the strong evidence, both that Mark's socioeconomic location was marginal and that his sociolinguistic world was limited.

Indirect Literary Influence and Common Cultural Conventions

Arguments that Mark was not likely to have received a classical education, however, do not discount the very real possibility that Mark indeed may have employed many literary and oral conventions that were characteristic of Homer. But it is more likely that the author would have done so through indirect, rather than direct, influence. In Mark's telling of the healing of the deaf man (7:31-37) and of the blind man (8:22–26), the two narratives contain shared vocabulary, shared order and structure, and a shared procedure for healing, followed by the shared admonition to silence. Joel Marcus lays out the comparison in chart form that I have roughly reproduced:

description of trip: (Mark 7:32–37)	description of trip: (Mark 8:22–26)
32a and they brought him (καὶ φέρουσιν αὐτῷ) a deaf man	22b and they brought him (καὶ φέρουσιν αὐτῷ) a blind man
32b and they beseeched him that (καὶ παρακαλοῦσιν αὐτὸν ἵνα) he lay his hand on him	22c and they beseeched him that (καὶ παρακαλοῦσιν αὐτὸν ἵνα) he lay his hand on him
33a and taking (ἀπολαβόμενος) him away	23a and taking (ἐπιλαβόμενος) his hand he led him out of

---

New York: Doubleday; New Haven: Yale University Press, 2000–2009), 1:60–61 and Watson, "*Life of Aesop.*"

from the crowd privately	the village
33b he put his fingers into his ears	23c and spitting (καὶ πτύσας) on his eyes he put his hands on him
33c and spitting (καὶ πτύσας) he touched his tongue	24a and looking up (καὶ ἀναβλέψας)
34a and looking up (καὶ ἀναβλέψας) to heaven	24b he [the blind man] said . . .
34c he [Jesus] . . . said . . .	*healing:*
healing:	26 and he sent him back to his house saying, 'Do not even go into the village.' [21]
36a and he commanded them not to tell anyone.	

The above example shows that Mark indeed employed literary conventions that were likely standard tropes of his sociolinguistic world. However, direct literary borrowing is not necessary to posit employment of literary conventions nor is the attainment of a classical education.

One need not posit direct literary borrowing at all, in fact. Think, for instance, of the well-known literary conventions that are available to us today. We attend plays, expecting the tension of protagonist played against antagonist; we read romances, expecting that the hero and heroine will "live happily ever after"; we watch TV series, expecting sexual tension between the male and female protagonists; we expect foreshadowing and retrospect. We expect letters to begin: "Dear So-and-so," and to end, "Sincerely," signed by the writer. All of these are literary or genre-specific conventions, but none of these conventions requires a literate audience for the genre or a classically trained expert to employ these conventions. There is no reason to assume that things would have been different in the ancient Mediterranean. Thus, rather than direct literary borrowing, it is much more plausible that

---

[21] Based on the construction by Marcus, *Mark*, 1:476.

our socially marginalized and linguistically inept friend, Mark, would have employed well-known oral and literary conventions available to him through public performances and storytelling rather than through classical conventions of mimesis.[22]

In some sense, MacDonald's own excellent research on the ubiquity of Homeric literary conventions in the Gospel writers' era poses the greatest direct challenge to his other claim of direct literary borrowing. It is this widespread access to Homer, which MacDonald persuasively demonstrates, that makes very plausible a contention that Mark indeed would have had access to Homer, but that it would have been indirect, rather than direct, access. I leave the reader, then, with a proposal: Perhaps more appropriate criteria to ensure claims of direct, rather than indirect, borrowing would require greater rigor and would entail more specific evidence. One example might be uncovering literary borrowing of more uniquely Homeric literary elements—for instance, Homer's characteristic use of epithets,[23] or epic similes,[24] or examples of efforts to mimic Homer's poetic meter. An analysis of the Gospels that could demonstrate these types of literary borrowings would offer the kind of support that would make Dennis MacDonald's contributions truly groundbreaking. As is, however, MacDonald's contributions are highly significant. Because of him, no study of the New Testament henceforth can ignore the classical literature of ancient Greece. This alone is a monumental contribution to the academic study of the New Testament.

---

[22] For further examples of Mark's use of such standard conventions, see Marcus, *Mark*, 1:198, 389.

[23] E.g., "swift-footed Achilles," "white-armed Andromache," "fair-haired Menelaus."

[24] E.g., "As the generation of leaves, so is that of humanity" (*Il.* 6.146); "He fell on them as a wave falls on a swift ship" (*Il.* 15.624).

SBL Panel Papers on The Dionysian Gospel

Neos Dionysos *in Textual and Cultural Mimesis*
Richard C. Miller

I wish to introduce myself as a since-graduated doctoral student who had the privilege to have Prof. MacDonald as my dissertation supervisor at the Claremont Graduate University School of Religion. While at Yale, I singled out Prof. MacDonald as the scholar, above all others, under whom I wished to study. As is all the more apparent today, he stood out as the one scholar most substantially dedicated to contextualizing fully the New Testament within the lively inferential world of cosmopolitan classical culture. New Testament scholarship has long neglected the broader contextual domain of ancient Greek and Latin culture, instead fundamentally restricting itself to the tide pool of earliest Christian and early Jewish writings, rather than wading and venturing out into the sea of Hellenistic and Roman literature whence most of the linguistic conventions and cultural codes inscribed and contested in the New Testament derive.

Even the similitude of the tide pool, however, fails by understating the circumstance inasmuch as earliest Christianity arose as a cross-current within the dominant centers of antique Mediterranean society, leveraging, upsetting, and frequently overturning the institutions of those presiding cultural structures. Indeed, the four Gospels survive as relics of that complex transaction precisely due to their success. Even the early Jewish strands of these traditions, once having met their complex appropriation within the Gospels, achieved a distinctly early Christian quality and found their traction, their cultural-linguistic purchase within these hubs of cosmopolitan urban culture. Prof. MacDonald has, at a most rudimentary level, shaped his entire scholarly career around this fundamental awareness, providing a profound debt not yet fully realized to the field.

The Dionysian Gospel among the Unlettered

His latest academic installment, *The Dionysian Gospel*, follows much of his signature methodological repertoire.[25] This may be loosely divided into two large portions, specifically a detailed source-critical analysis of the fourth Gospel and a mimesis-critical analysis contending for Euripides' *Bacchae* as John's principal antetext. From my first encounters with MacDonald's work nearly fifteen years ago, I have long appreciated each of his books as a grand chest filled with many gems and intricate treasures. I had much of the same edifying, venturesome feeling while reading *The Dionysian Gospel*. Approached in that manner, his work never disappoints.

Regrettably, however, as I read through the manuscript, the thought rose to my head, "Oh, here goes another great MacDonald contribution that the field is sorely deficient to embrace." As I have spoken with numerous critics of his work over the years, I have discerned two causes underlying this phenomenon of reluctance. First, the academy does not know how to read a book. We are all trained to be black-belt critics, to find the weak point in the argument, and to topple the whole apple cart with one well-placed critical blow. Instead of treasure hunting, as it were, we find some useless satisfaction in dismembering any thesis by pointing out its weakest link. Thus, most who have read and rejected MacDonald's arguments do so by being caught in the proverbial weeds of ancillary argumentation. This leads to the other cause of impediment, an altogether sad, pandemic-level lack of training and familiarity with classical culture in the

---

[25] Dennis R. MacDonald, *The Dionysian Gospel: The Fourth Gospel and Euripides* (Minneapolis: Fortress, 2017).

Romano-Greek East, specifically respecting those cities that bore the earliest Christian movements, the Hellenistic urban centers of ancient cultural production, rich contexts altogether enchanted by Greek linguism.

Shamefully, only a handful of New Testament scholars today have the slightest familiarity with Euripides, the veritable George Lucas of classical antique culture. By textual evidence, the playwright was one of the most canonized authors of Mediterranean antiquity, following only the towering figures of Homer and Hesiod. His *Bacchae* stood as the longest running, most broadly popular play of the Greek East. It was the *Star Wars* of classical antiquity. One would have to have lived in an island cave not to have been familiar with the performed tragedy.

Textual and Cultural Mimesis

I found especially compelling MacDonald's more clearly nuanced methodological approach. In *The Dionysian Gospel*, MacDonald's argument proves more formidable by carrying a broader domain of mimesis, not merely syntagmatic, textual mimesis (as has often characterized his past work), but also cultural, formal mimesis (i.e., related to the iconified figure Dionysus). This shift abides well with a strong understanding of mimetic cognition, particularly with regard to a performed work. As my own monograph has laid out, from a semiotic standpoint, the convention or custom of deification relied upon the display of mimetic signals related to specific archetypal figures established early in the tradition.[26] Of these, a select few served as archetypal demigods, supplying the semiotic narrational patterns of the tradition. This special list typically included Heracles, Dionysus, Castor and Pollux, Asclepius, and Romulus, the

---

[26] Richard C. Miller, *Resurrection and Reception in Early Christianity* (Routledge Studies in Religion 44; New York: Routledge, 2015).

premiere iconic figures of classical antiquity whom Anton Elter described as "ein bestimmter Kanon von Halbgöttern."[27] In his *De natura deorum*, Cicero explicitly explained the policy, listing the archetypes (2.24):

> Human manner and community custom have established that they, as regards fame and disposition, raise up to heaven persons of distinguished benefaction. Thus, Hercules, Castor and Pollux, Aesculapius, Liber (i.e., Dionysus), . . . and Romulus, the same one whom they regard as Quirinus, with their souls enduring and enjoying eternal life, are fittingly regarded as gods, since they are the very best and are immortal.

Arthur Darby Nock's 1928 article "Notes on Ruler-Cult" described the language and nature of such associations, particularly as related to Hellenistic and Roman ruler imagery.[28] Nock, for instance, provided a substantive section on the appellation neos Dionysos, a title applied to such figures as Mithridates IV, Ptolemy XII, Ptolemy XIII, Mark Antony, Gaius, Trajan, Hadrian, Antinous, Antoninus Pius, and Commodus. *Imitatio Bacchi*, particularly when applied to the Hellenistic and Roman rulers, by extension likewise signaled candidacy for the imperial legacy of Alexander, that is, *imitatio Alexandri*, as oriental conqueror and world ruler. The designation "*neos*" expands, however, to include the full range of archetypal figures and may apply, in substitution, a variety of interchangeable terms, such as *kainos, heteros, allos, deuteros,* and *hoploteros*. Nock's article, moreover, likewise becomes instructive in recalling that the *imitatio* of these

---

[27] Anton Elter, *Donarum Pateras (Horat. Carm. 4.8)*, Programm zur Feier des Gedächtnisses des Stifters der Universität Königs Friedrich Wilhelm III, (Bonn: C. Georgi, 1907), 40.

[28] Arthur Darby Nock, "Notes on Ruler-Cult, I–IV," *JHS* 48.1 (1928): 21–43.

archetypal figures did not imply an ontological identification or equivalency. After careful survey and analysis, Nock concludes, "There is not, therefore, in general a definite popular belief that a particular ruler is in a strict sense the reincarnation of a particular deity."[29]

The Gospel of John as Asceticized Bacchanalia

There may be quite some difficulty in observing any sizeable semantic distance between *pistis* and *gnosis* in earliest Christian tradition, inasmuch as both terms chiefly implied the assertion of otherwise unwarranted inferences in the face of inadequate or contrary data. MacDonald reveals that this feature of the Johannine idiom (i.e., the distinctive social language of the Johannine tradition) had its roots in a shared metanarrative with the *Bacchae*. The author of the Johannine epilogue sought to persuade that Jesus (the mundane itinerate sayings figure of Palestine) was the son of the Judeo-Christian god (John 20:31), thus strategically merging the two most primitive Christian traditions. As the narrative's antagonist, the Theban king Pentheus functioned as a metonym of unbelief (specifically regarding the divinity of the incarnate Dionysus), a cardinal moral flaw which spelled his ultimate tragic demise. MacDonald's analysis reveals John's nimble strumming of these Bacchic themes and motifs, powerfully invoking the play's supremely tragic lesson. MacDonald persuasively demonstrates the functional/mimetic relation of the Bacchae's prologue with John's prologue. Members of the earliest Christians of the Johannine school found their analogues with the Bacchants, that is, in asceticized cultural adaptation.

The Dionysian Gospel thus crafts an asceticized Bacchanalia, a Jewish wedding at Cana wherein the Christian

---

[29] Nock, "Notes on Ruler-Cult," 35.

demigod performs the signature Bacchic miracle: water turned to vast quantities of wine. As with the Messianic Secret of Mark, the Johannine storyboard is festooned with Dionysian epiphany motifs. Although decorating the narrative in numerous, at times more subtle ways, MacDonald finds stories such as the Woman at the Well and Jesus's Trial to provide more overt mimetic undertones. Standing back, MacDonald convincingly describes a single governing common (mimetic) theme: both describe a feral, unstoppable divine movement that transcends and defies government institution and conventional order.

MacDonald's work recalibrates our appreciation of Hellenistic signification in John's Gospel, that is, the work's stylized display of Hellenic literary and cultural *savoir faire*, the very defining essence of Hellenism in the ancient Greek East. Such sophistication in John obtains as a referential bricolage of adapted, culturally charged images drawn from the very canons of Hellenism. One may also include, for instance, references to martyrdom of Socrates, as Jesus prepares his disciples for his own chosen death, as well as the provocative invocation of the Greek philosophical schools via Jesus as the incarnation of Logos, the demiurgos of creation. In the end, however, we may expect undue resistance to MacDonald's argument in *The Dionysian Gospel* due to what I observe as an inappropriate effort in the West to legitimate through the academy its premodern mythic traditions against the tide of science. An accurate, humanistic study of John, one that further deconstructs the primitive roots of the early Christian mythosystem, frightens many. In his pioneering spirit, MacDonald again leads on, undaunted.

John's Politics of Imitation
Chan Sok Park

Dennis MacDonald's book *The Dionysian Gospel: The Fourth Gospel and Euripides* can be situated in two main areas of research within the current trends in Johannine studies. The first is the increasing scholarly interest about ancient drama — including Greek tragedy — as a useful literary context in which the Fourth Gospel may be read. While many scholars have discussed the dramatic character of the Fourth Gospel, their use and understanding of the term "drama" have been divergent. Some explore a genre of tragedy strictly as explicated in Aristotle's *Poetics* for their studies of the Fourth Gospel. Others take the word "dramatic" rather freely to assess John's literary qualities without engaging in any actual discussion of ancient Greek drama. The recent works by Jo-Ann Brant, George Parsenios, and Harold Attridge have made convincing cases of the Fourth Gospel as a "dramatic" text in a more balanced way.[1] By exploring the ways in which John artistically demonstrates various ancient dramatic techniques, these scholars have claimed that this Gospel tells its own story of Jesus's life and death in the guise of the dramatic genre. MacDonald's present work pushes one step further: it thoroughly examines the affinities between the Fourth Gospel

---

[1] Jo-Ann A. Brant, *Dialogue and Drama: Elements of Greek Tragedy in the Fourth Gospel* (Peabody, MA: Hendrickson, 2004); George L. Parsenios, *Departure and Consolation: The Johannine Farewell Discourses in Light of Greco-Roman Literature* (NovTSup 117; Leiden: Brill, 2005); George L. Parsenios, *Rhetoric and Drama in the Johannine Lawsuit Motif* (WUNT I/258; Tübingen: Mohr Siebeck, 2010); and Harold W. Attridge, "Genre," *How John Works: Storytelling in the Fourth Gospel* (ed. Douglas Estes and Ruth Sheridan; Atlanta: SBL, 2016), 7–22.

and a specific work of drama, Euripides' *Bacchae*, both in terms of shared characterizations and plots.

The second area of current Johannine research related to this book is how to handle the complex composition theory of John's Gospel. In recent years, scholars generally tend to focus on the Gospel in its final form while paying less attention to possible sources or redactional processes at work behind the text.[2] MacDonald's work does not shy away from the challenging diachronic disputes and instead offers an innovative hypothesis of the development of Johannine writings. Any theory of Johannine compositions has to be provisional, but, as MacDonald puts it, it is definitely a worthwhile task, one at which his study succeeds.

For both of the above reasons, *The Dionysian Gospel* makes a significant contribution to Johannine studies in particular and the study of the New Testament and Greco-Roman literature in general. This work invites readers of the Fourth Gospel to reconsider its place within a literary history of the Johannine tradition and its literary relation to ancient Greek tragedy, particularly Euripides' *Bacchae*. It is hoped that the comments and questions that follow will promote a lively and useful conversation about this important book.

Politics of Imitation

The first question pertains to what the classicist Tim Whitmarsh calls the "politics of imitation (*mimēsis*)."[3] In his important work on Greek sophistic literature of the Roman Empire, Whitmarsh examines a politics of imitation as its main characteristic. In his view, Greek imperial literature is "not a reflex of a pre-existing Greek identity, but precisely the

---

[2] A notable exception is Urban C. von Wahlde, *The Gospel and Letters of John* (3 vols.; ECC; Grand Rapids: Eerdmans, 2010).

[3] Tim Whitmarsh, *Greek Literature and the Roman Empire: The Politics of Imitation* (Oxford: Oxford University Press, 2001).

space in which identity is constructed and disseminated."⁴ In *The Dionysian Gospel*, MacDonald makes a strong case for a conscious literary connection between the earliest version of the Johannine Gospel and Euripides' the *Bacchae*. This leads to a question: What would have prompted the Fourth Evangelist to craft a type of biographical narrative of Jesus as a rival to Dionysus, particularly the one depicted in the *Bacchae,* in the first place?⁵ As MacDonald convincingly presents, there is no doubt about the popularity and influence of the *Bacchae* throughout antiquity, so it is not surprising at all to see the *Bacchae* serving as a literary model. The question at hand is rather about the politics of imitation.

At least in passing, MacDonald presents a brief explanation of this connection between the two texts. In chapter 2, he states, "The Johannine author apparently thought that the Jesus depicted in the Synoptics *could not compete with* Dionysus as a benefactor to his followers, who, according to Euripides, provided wine, rejuvenation, water, and eternal life. *By imitating*—rather, by emulating or rivaling the god of the *Bacchae*—the Evangelist supplemented the earlier Gospels with a god who offered 'gift after gift.'"⁶ What, then, would propel the Johannine author(s) to care about Dionysus in the first place? MacDonald also claims that his study of comparison between John and the *Bacchae* is "to demonstrate that the Johannine Evangelist not only imitated Euripides, he [sic] expected his readers to esteem Jesus as greater than Dionysus."⁷ Does this mean that one form of the Jesus movement (i.e., Johannine Christianity) in the earliest formative period grew out of, or had been formed in

---

⁴ Whitmarsh, *Greek Literature and the Roman Empire*, 32.

⁵ For similar concerns, see Michael Kochenash, "Even Good Homer Nods," *supra*.

⁶ MacDonald, *Dionysian Gospel*, 61; italics mine.

⁷ MacDonald, *Dionysian Gospel*, 27.

competition with, the contemporaneous Dionysus cults? Or does it suggest that the Jesus story itself originated in the bowels of Dionysiac myth? What is the earliest Fourth Evangelist's "politics of imitation"?

Mimetic Christian Identity in Luke-Acts and John

Related to this first question, in his previous work entitled *Luke and Vergil,* MacDonald also argued for the influence of Euripides' *Bacchae* in Luke-Acts.[8] There, he highlighted the four extended sequences in Luke-Acts imitating the *Bacchae*: (1) Jesus's activities at Jericho (Luke 18:35–19:10); (2) Peter's activities after Pentecost (Acts 2–5); (3) Saul's role as a theomachos (Acts 9:1–19a); and (4) Paul's presentation as a new Dionysus (Acts 16).[9] The last example is particularly interesting, as it describes Paul's prison-breaks in comparison with Euripides' Dionysus.

If this is the case, then two major early Jesus movements—those reflected in Luke-Acts and John—used Euripides' Dionysus as a literary model to present the two major characters in their foundational stories: Paul and Jesus respectively. Indeed, in chapter 2 of *The Dionysian Gospel*, MacDonald states, "it would be tempting to postulate that Luke's imitations of the *Bacchae* inspired additional imitations in the earliest Johannine Gospel."[10] How, then, should we evaluate the significance of Euripides' Dionysus for the process of constructing early Christian identities?

---

[8] Dennis R. MacDonald, *Luke and Vergil: Imitations of Classical Greek Literature* (NTGL 2; Lanham, MD: Rowman & Littlefield, 2015), 11–65. See also Ilseo Park, "Acts 2 as an Intertextual Map: Moving from Dionysian to Platonic Identity," *infra* and Michael Kochenash, "The Scandal of Gentile Inclusion: Reading Acts 17 with Euripides' *Bacchae*," *infra*.

[9] MacDonald, *Luke and Vergil*, 20.

[10] MacDonald, *Dionysian Gospel*, 113–14.

Absence of the Lord's Supper

The third question relates to the significance for this work of the absence of the Lord's Supper in John's Gospel. It is unclear whether John knew the story of the Last Supper as is found in the Synoptics and 1 Cor 11. However, there can be little doubt that John's Gospel had its own theological stance on the presence and power of Christ in some form of Eucharist, as evidenced in chapter 6 (Jesus as the bread of life), chapter 15 (Jesus as the vine), and—probably a later addition to the rest of the Gospel—chapter 21 (Jesus's resurrection meal). What is striking about John's account of the Last Supper in chapters 13-17 is, then, that the institution of the Eucharist or Lord's Supper is not referenced here. Instead of Jesus's memorable words about the bread and wine in his last meal with disciples, John uniquely depicts a highly symbolic act of washing disciples' feet, accompanied by Jesus's command to serve one another in the same way (13:1-20).

Given the strong presence of wine in the Last Supper, does this omission in John have any implications for MacDonald's proposal? It should be noted that he does not include in the reconstructed Dionysian Gospel significant portions of the Johannine farewell discourses except the "I am the true grapevine" saying in chapter 15 and a few others.[11] Does the lack of any account of the Eucharist in John's story of the Last Supper make any differences in MacDonald's proposed thesis of John as a Dionysian Gospel? Or is there an explanation for this absence in John that arises out of the perspective of the proposed thesis of this book?

Johannine Literature and the Johannine Community

The last question concerns the idea of "community" in this work. MacDonald's new proposed history of the Johannine literary tradition is particularly fascinating. Clearly,

---

[11] MacDonald, *Dionysian Gospel*, 194-95.

its primary focus lies in a literary history of Johannine writings, rather than a reconstruction of the history of the so-called Johannine community. Yet, the term "Johannine community" appears throughout this book. Occasionally remarks appear related to a possible history of the Johannine community in light of the proposed literary history of Johannine writings. For example, chapter 3 "shows how a later hand rewrote this Dionysian Gospel as a response to the expulsion of Johannine believers from Jewish Synagogues."[12] This statement is reminiscent of the classical model of the history of Johannine community proposed by J. Louis Martin.[13] While the notion of a Johannine community has become so thoroughly engrained in scholarship on the Fourth Gospel, reasonable questions have been raised about the reconstructed history of this hypothetical community, as well as the assumptions involved with reading the Gospel as a reflection of a particular community.[14] So, what is the meaning of "Johannine community" when used in this book? Does MacDonald's work propose, at least implicitly, a possible history of Johannine Christianity based on a literary history of Johannine writings?

It was a great pleasure to read this insightful work. I hope that the comments and questions above foster discussions about its significance and potential impact on Johannine scholarship more broadly.

---

[12] MacDonald, *Dionysian Gospel*, xvi.

[13] See, e.g., J. Louis Martyn, *History and Theology in the Fourth Gospel* (3rd ed.; NTL; Louisville: Westminster John Knox, 2003).

[14] For the issue of deploying the notion of "community" in early Christian studies, see Stanley Stowers, "The Concept of 'Community' and the History of Early Christianity," *MTSR* 23.3 (2011): 238–56.

The First Dionysian Gospel: Imitational and Redactional Layers in Luke and John
Mark G. Bilby

The First Edition of John as the Dionysian Gospel

When first reading through the unpublished draft of MacDonald's *The Dionysian Gospel*, I was admittedly skeptical about such a provocative title.[1] The frequent use of the phrase "the Dionysian Gospel" throughout the book did not alleviate this skepticism.[2] My initial inclination was to wonder if this was too presumptuous a label or even a not-so-subtle method of persuasion that repeated the premise in short form until the reader unconsciously accepted it.[3] But with the whole volume in hindsight, and the criteria for intertextuality thoroughly met between John and Euripides' *Bacchae*, I became convinced that "the Dionysian Gospel" is an altogether apt title for the first edition of John. Both on its own terms and in comparison to other early Gospels, John is indeed *the* Dionysian Gospel.

Numerous and dense parallels rise to the level of highly probable to certain indications of dependence on the *Bacchae* of Euripides. Such dependence can be seen in a wide range of ways, from identical and unique word choice, to themes and dramatic settings, to character developments and plot twists. Like Dionysus, Jesus is a god who comes to earth

---

[1] Dennis R. MacDonald, *The Dionysian Gospel: The Fourth Gospel and Euripides* (Minneapolis: Fortress, 2017).

[2] MacDonald, *Dionysian Gospel*, xvi, 50, 59, 61, 64, etc.

[3] The latter view was prompted in part by uses of "Dionysian Gospel" even when no clear mimetic parallel was noted, e.g., Peter's lack of remorse. MacDonald, *Dionysian Gospel*, 89.

in mortal disguise.[4] He has a champion heralding him.[5] The people's leaders reject him.[6] His symbolic names abound.[7] Jesus's first, stage-setting miracle is clearly a Dionysian one; both bring forth wine miraculously.[8] Yet that is only one of numerous, identity-establishing miracles that the two share in common. Jesus and Dionysus both make old men move as if they are young again.[9] Both prompt devotion from old men in spite of competing family loyalties.[10] The Johannine Jesus provides his own miraculous supply of water and attracts women followers known for their promiscuity, just as Dionysus was famed to do.[11] Both vex their initiates/disciples with the requirement of eating the god's raw flesh and drinking his blood.[12] *Iesus Dionysos* is harshly interrogated as to his provenance and paternity.[13] He is the liberator of slaves.[14] He is the one whom his opponents cannot see but the formerly blind clearly can.[15] He is the one who can miraculously escape arrest.[16] He is the one whose initiates travel safely into the underworld and are brought back to life.[17] Jesus and Dionysus are similarly opposed by god-fighters.[18] Yet both are equally acclaimed by many groups of

---

[4] MacDonald, *Dionysian Gospel*, 28–29, 30–32.
[5] MacDonald, *Dionysian Gospel*, 29.
[6] MacDonald, *Dionysian Gospel*, 29–30.
[7] MacDonald, *Dionysian Gospel*, 38–40.
[8] MacDonald, *Dionysian Gospel*, 40–44, 67.
[9] MacDonald, *Dionysian Gospel*, 46–49.
[10] MacDonald, *Dionysian Gospel*, 48–49.
[11] MacDonald, *Dionysian Gospel*, 51–55.
[12] MacDonald, *Dionysian Gospel*, 64–67.
[13] MacDonald, *Dionysian Gospel*, 68–71, 89–95.
[14] MacDonald, *Dionysian Gospel*, 71–73.
[15] MacDonald, *Dionysian Gospel*, 73–75.
[16] MacDonald, *Dionysian Gospel*, 75–76.
[17] MacDonald, *Dionysian Gospel*, 79–81.
[18] MacDonald, *Dionysian Gospel*, 81–82.

people.[19] Jesus imitates Dionysus even as he rivals him as the true grapevine.[20] Both willingly meet their own arrest.[21] Though the ignominy of the crucifixion and lack of vengeance are uncharacteristic of Dionysus, the Johannine Jesus still plays a *Bacchae*-inspired role in his imitation of Pentheus, the murdered king.[22] The Johannine resurrection interweaves characteristics of Dionysus and Pentheus in its depiction of the defiled, royal corpse being raised within a garden and women followers who surround him but also do not initially recognize his body.[23] The disembodied apotheosis of the first edition of John is hallmark Dionysus.[24]

Other adduced parallels run the gamut from uncertain to puzzling. In these occasions, it may simply be that MacDonald knows these texts far better than readers like I do and that he sees connections that have to be explained point by point to the uninitiated. For example, Mary's anointing of the feet of Jesus is adduced as John's depiction of Jesus as "a different kind of lover from Dionysus."[25] Yes, Jesus is a murdered king like Pentheus, but why is it that Mary Magdalene rather than Mary the Mother plays the part of the mother of Pentheus, who cannot recognize her son's body?[26] Caveats notwithstanding, these minor quibbles and questions do not impair MacDonald's Dionysian argument in the least.

---

[19] MacDonald, *Dionysian Gospel*, 82–83.
[20] MacDonald, *Dionysian Gospel*, 83–85.
[21] MacDonald, *Dionysian Gospel*, 85–87.
[22] MacDonald, *Dionysian Gospel*, 96–100.
[23] MacDonald, *Dionysian Gospel*, 102–08.
[24] MacDonald, *Dionysian Gospel*, 108–09.
[25] MacDonald, *Dionysian Gospel*, 79.
[26] MacDonald, *Dionysian Gospel*, 102–08.

Dependencies between Editions of John and (Editions of) Luke

It is extremely impressive that at the same time MacDonald has pioneered seminal, comprehensive resources for mimesis criticism, he has also concurrently in these same books and in others undertaken an exhaustive and fresh account of the content and order of Q (or rather, Q+/Papias), the Synoptic Problem, the redactional layers of the Gospel of John, the interrelationships of Johannine literature more broadly, and the place of Revelation in the Johannine corpus. These enormously fruitful yields are rooted in a lifetime's cultivation of brilliant scholarship. It will take years for this careful work to ferment throughout the scholarly community.

Many of the arguments and reconstructions put forward are as convincing as they are ingenious. For example, the Gospel of John was composed in three editions, 2–3 John were written before 1 John, the Johannine epistles convey a clear knowledge of Matthew, and the Johannine corpus was jointly redacted and formed a distinct literary collection prior to the imposition of the four-Gospel canon.[27]

Among these ambitious and thoroughgoing reconstructions, the one I found to be most problematic was the relationship of John to Luke. Throughout *The Dionysian Gospel*, MacDonald repeatedly claims that the Gospel of John (in all three of its major redactional stages) was written after Luke and Acts and depends upon them. Together with Acts, Luke is depicted as the creation of a singular moment in history rather than as a text that evinces at least two major stages of composition.

In this regard, it should be noted that MacDonald's dates for the joint composition of Luke and Acts have become more narrow in *The Dionysian Gospel* in contrast to what he postulated in the two earlier books of his mimetic trilogy: *The*

---

[27] MacDonald, *Dionysian Gospel*, 137–71.

Gospels and Homer and *Luke and Vergil*.[28] Previously, MacDonald left open a wider range of dates for Luke-Acts: 115–130 CE.[29] But this range of dates for Luke-Acts suddenly narrowed in *The Dionysian Gospel* to 115 CE, apparently to fit his precise dating of the first edition of John and the final redactions of John, Revelation, and the Johannine corpus between 120–130 CE.[30] Here we reproduce MacDonald's most recent list of dates for the compositional and redactional history of the Gospels and their key sources:[31]

- Q+ (*Logoi of Jesus*), ca. 60–66;
- Mark, ca. 75–80;
- Matthew, ca. 80–90;
- 2, 3, and 1 John and Rev. 1:10–22:7, ca. 90–100;
- Papias's *Exposition*, ca. 110;
- Luke-Acts, ca. 115;
- John 1–20 (first edition), ca. 117;
- 2nd and 3rd editions of John (including chapter 21), final redaction of Revelation, and creation of Johannine corpus, ca. 120–130.

The date of 115 CE and Trajanic setting for Luke-Acts does comply with Richard I. Pervo's *terminus post quem* for Acts,[32] but it is certainly more narrow than what is typically found among others scholars who have concluded on a

---

[28] Dennis R. MacDonald, *The Gospels and Homer: Imitations of Greek Epic in Mark and Luke-Acts* (NTGL 1; Lanham, MD: Rowman & Littlefield, 2015) and *Luke and Vergil: Imitations of Classical Greek Literature* (NTGL 2; Lanham, MD: Rowman & Littlefield, 2015).

[29] MacDonald, *Gospels and Homer*, 20 and MacDonald, *Luke and Vergil*, 6, 226.

[30] MacDonald, *Dionysian Gospel*, 169.

[31] MacDonald, *Dionysian Gospel*, 169.

[32] Richard I. Pervo, *Dating Acts: Between the Evangelists and the Apologists* (Santa Rosa, CA: Polebridge, 2006), who dates Acts in the 110s. See also Mikeal C. Parsons, *Acts* (Paideia; Grand Rapids: Baker Academic, 2008), 16–17, who dates Acts around 110 CE.

second-century date for the canonical version of Luke and/or the composition of Acts.³³ My own analysis of Luke aligns with those who locate an early version of Luke in the late first century (ca. 80–100 CE) and its final/canonical version well

---

³³ John Knox, *Marcion and the New Testament: An Essay in the Early History of the Canon* (Chicago: University of Chicago Press, 1942), 114–39; J. C. O'Neill, *The Theology of Acts in Its Historical Settings* (London: SPCK, 1961), 1–63; Christopher Mount, *Pauline Christianity: Luke-Acts and the Legacy of Paul* (NovTSup 104; Leiden: Brill, 2002); Joseph B. Tyson, "The Date of Acts: A Reconsideration," *Forum* n.s. 5.1 (2002): 33–51; Mary Rose D'Angelo, "The ANHP Question in Luke-Acts: Imperial Masculinity and the Deployment of Women in the Early Second Century," *A Feminist Companion to Luke* (ed. Amy-Jill Levine; Feminist Companion to the New Testament and Early Christian Writings 3; Sheffield: Sheffield Academic Press, 2002), 44–69; Joseph B. Tyson, "Why Dates Matter: The Case of the Acts of the Apostles," *The Fourth R* 18.2 (2005): 8–14; Matthias Klinghardt, "Markion vs. Lukas: Plädoyer für die Wiederaufnahme eines alten Falles," *NTS* 52.4 (2006): 484–513; Joseph B. Tyson, *Marcion and Luke-Acts: A Defining Struggle* (Columbia: University of South Carolina Press, 2006); Laura Nasrallah, "The Acts of the Apostles, Greek Cities, and Hadrian's Panhellenion," *JBL* 127.3 (2008): 533–66; Shelly Matthews, *Perfect Martyr: The Stoning of Stephen and the Construction of Christian Identity* (Oxford: Oxford University Press, 2010); *Acts and Christian Beginnings: The Acts Seminar Report* (ed. Dennis E. Smith and Joseph B. Tyson; Salem, OR: Polebridge, 2013); *Engaging Early Christian History: Reading Acts in the Second Century* (ed. Rubén R. Dupertuis and Todd Penner; London: Routledge, 2014); John S. Kloppenborg, "Literate Media in Early Christ Groups: The Creation of a Christian Book Culture," *JECS* 22.1 (2014), 21–59; Mark G. Bilby, "Pliny's Correspondence and the Acts of the Apostles: An Intertextual Relationship," *Luke on Jesus, Paul and Christianity: What Did He Really Know?* (ed. Joseph Verheyden and John S. Kloppenborg; BTS 29; Leuven: Peeters, 2017), 147–69; Thomas E. Phillips, "How Did Paul Become a Roman 'Citizen'? Reading Acts in Light of Pliny the Younger," *Luke on Jesus, Paul and Christianity: What Did He Really Know?* (ed. Joseph Verheyden and John S. Kloppenborg; BTS 29; Leuven: Peeters, 2017), 171–89; Shelly Matthews, "Does Dating Luke-Acts into the Second Century Affect the Q Hypothesis?" *Gospel Interpretation and the Q-Hypothesis* (ed. Mogens Müller and Heike Omerzu; LNTS 573; London: Bloomsbury T&T Clark, 2018), 245–66.

into the second century (ca. 117–150 CE). With this in mind, let us proceed to evaluate the direction and significance of the parallels between Luke and John.

MacDonald consistently maps parallels between Luke and John as traveling in one direction, from Luke to John. Some of these are reasonable:

- John 11:1–2 conflates Luke 7:37–38 (sinful woman wipes Jesus's feet), Luke 10:38–39 ("village," "Mary" and "Martha"), and Luke 16:20a ("Lazarus");[34]
- John 13:3–5, 12–17 depends on Luke 12:37–38 (Jesus as servant);[35]
- John 13:16 depends on Luke 22:24–27 (meal instructions about rank);[36]
- John 20:17, 25, 27 depends on Luke 24:37–39 (clarifying that the resurrected body of Jesus could be touched);[37]

To these, I would also add that John 8:58b–59 and 10:39 are likely dependent on Luke 4:29–30 (Jesus escaping arrest/death). MacDonald connects these verses but does not clearly claim a dependent relationship.[38]

In other dependencies adduced by MacDonald, it seems just as reasonable—if not more so—to posit Mark as John's source rather than Luke.

- John 20:1, Mark 16:1, and Luke 24:1 ("first day of the Sabbath");[39]
- John 20:1, Mark 16:1, and Luke 24:10 (Mary Magdalene).[40]

---

[34] MacDonald, *Dionysian Gospel*, 77.
[35] MacDonald, *Dionysian Gospel*, 147.
[36] MacDonald, *Dionysian Gospel*, 149.
[37] MacDonald, *Dionysian Gospel*, 105, 108, 118, 201 n. 99.
[38] MacDonald, *Dionysian Gospel*, 75.
[39] MacDonald, *Dionysian Gospel*, 103.

In yet other examples, all of which are unattested by Marcion and several of which belong to the famed "Western Non-Interpolations" of Luke 24, the direction of dependence more likely runs from John to Luke rather than *vice versa*:[41]

- Luke 4:9b–10 depends on John 1:49, 51b ("son of god" ... "angels");[42]
- Luke 3:20b depends on John 3:24 ("John" ... "in prison");[43]
- Luke 22:3a depends on John 13:27 ("Satan" entering "Judas");[44]
- Luke 24:12 depends on John 20:3, 11 ("stooping" to see in the tomb);[45]
- Luke 24:36 depends on John 20:19, 21, 26 ("peace be with you"; see also John 14:27);[46]
- Luke 24:40 depends on John 20:20 (Jesus reveals his stigmata).

To this list, I would also add one or two of the Lukan last sayings on the cross. Witnesses to Marcion's *Gospel* are ambiguous about Luke 23:34a, but they are clear that 23:43 was not present. The former possibly belongs to the later/canonical edition of Luke, while the latter likely does. The later inclusion of one or both probably took some inspiration from the three sayings from the cross in the first edition of John.

---

[40] MacDonald, *Dionysian Gospel*, 103.

[41] Michael Wade Martin, "Defending the 'Western Non-Interpolations': The Case for an Anti-Separationist *Tendenz* in the Longer Alexandrian Readings," *JBL* 124.2 (2005): 269–94. Cited approvingly by Matthews, "Does Dating Luke-Acts into the Second Century Affect the Q Hypothesis?", 248.

[42] MacDonald, *Dionysian Gospel*, 39–40.

[43] MacDonald, *Dionysian Gospel*, 60.

[44] MacDonald, *Dionysian Gospel*, 146.

[45] MacDonald, *Dionysian Gospel*, 103.

[46] MacDonald, *Dionysian Gospel*, 108–09, 201 n. 99.

Given the ambiguity of witnesses and disagreements among scholars, the direction of influence between Luke 24:42-43 and John 21:12, 15 (demonstration of Jesus eating post-resurrection) is difficult to discern. In regard to the relationship of John to Acts, however, MacDonald adduces two examples of dependence, both of which seem unlikely as traveling from Acts to John, but reasonable as traveling from John to Acts:

- John 18:20-21 and Acts 24:19-21 (Jesus and Paul speaking openly);[47]
- John 18:22-23 and Acts 23:2-4 (Jesus and Paul beaten).[48]

In his defense, MacDonald elsewhere does say that matters are "less certain" regarding "the Dionysian Evangelist" in regard to "his knowledge of Acts."[49]

The hypothesis that the direction of dependence only runs from a singular Luke-Acts to a multi-edition John carries a much bigger burden of proof than the specific caveats and counter-claims detailed above. The most significant argument against a singular direction of dependence is the unexplained absence of numerous distinctive Lukan materials from John. MacDonald hints at this gap in regard to the passion narratives and attempts to explain it as part of a consistent editorial strategy of John vis-à-vis the Synoptic Gospels:

> There should be no doubt that the Johannine Evangelist knew the narratives of Jesus's death from the Synoptics, but even a cursory comparison of the Passion Narratives reveals that John's Gospel lacks many of the elements that created pathos, irony, and complexity in the Synoptics.[50]

---

[47] MacDonald, *Dionysian Gospel*, 88.
[48] MacDonald, *Dionysian Gospel*, 88.
[49] MacDonald, *Dionysian Gospel*, 54.
[50] MacDonald, *Dionysian Gospel*, 87.

True as this is, the distinctive Lukan elements absent from John go far beyond the passion narrative and elements of "pathos, irony, and complexity." They include the entirety of the Lukan birth narratives (Luke 1-2). From the Lukan passion (Luke 23), John lacks the reappearing character of Herod, Pilate's threefold declaration of innocence, Luke's three last sayings on the cross, as well as the mourning crowds.

From the Lukan resurrection narratives, John is missing not only the Emmaus road story (24:13-35) but also the extended conclusion (24:44-53), which includes final instructions, opening the minds of the disciples to the scriptures, the Jerusalem-launched mission, the journey to Bethany, the ascension, and the disciples worshipping in the Jerusalem temple. To these obvious, large gaps, we may also add numerous examples of redactions *within* Lukan stories, stories that were used by John, but evidently in an earlier and simpler form.[51] Moreover, MacDonald's own mimetic discoveries further this argument, for John lacks any reference to Luke's imitations of Livy, Plutarch, Vergil, and Xenophon, as well as most if not all of Luke's distinctive mimetic responses to Plato.[52] Yes, the first edition of John used Luke,

---

[51] The story of the centurion's/official's son/servant at Capernaum (Luke 7:1-10 // John 4:46b-54) is an excellent example of this. John clearly depends on Luke rather than Matthew (8:5-13), and yet many of the features in Luke that are absent in Matthew are also absent from John, especially the praise of the centurion as the builder of the synagogue and the Jewish elders functioning as mediators of Jesus's communications with the Gentile official. These unique features in Luke likely reflect a later redaction, one unknown to the Dionysian Evangelist.

[52] In *The Dionysian Gospel*, MacDonald does not recount any imitations of the *Aeneid* or *Phaedo* found within John. However, he notes imitations of both the *Aeneid* and *Phaedo* in Luke within the pages of *Luke and Vergil*: v-ix, 7-8, 105-14, 126-27, 138-40, 147-48, 151-52, 156-59, 171-72, 174, 178-79, 183-85, 187-88, 191-92, 193-95, 196-99, 213-14, 217-18, 220-21.

but not the final/canonical version of Luke. The fairly narrow, *Bacchae*-focused mimetic project of the first edition of John attests to this, especially when contrasted with the far more expansive and eclectic mimetic project undertaken in the final version of Luke in concert with Acts. The later version of Luke likely drew upon John, even in its second or third version, as part of its thoroughgoing redaction of its own passion and resurrection narrative.

Marcion as a Redactional-Mimetic Pivot-Point

Missing from MacDonald's reconstructions are two vitally important pieces of the early-second-century puzzle: Marcion and Pliny. Both are crucial figures for diagramming the pivot points in the redactional histories of John and Luke-Acts.

Dieter Roth's painstaking critical edition of Marcion's *Gospel* has now made it possible to undertake a thoroughgoing redaction-critical analysis of the two major versions of Luke.[53] Recent scholarship on Marcion has confirmed that Marcion was not the pen-knifing editor or canonical innovator that his later detractors made him out to be.[54] His *Gospel* represented an early version of the Gospel that later came to be known by the name of Luke. Thus Marcion's reconstructed *Gospel* is the most significant external witness we have to this early version of Luke, and the variations between canonical Luke and

---

[53] Dieter T. Roth, *The Text of Marcion's Gospel* (NTTSD 49; Leiden: Brill, 2015).

[54] See Knox, *Marcion and the New Testament*; Jason D. BeDuhn, "The Myth of Marcion as Redactor: The Evidence of Marcion's Gospel against an Assumed Marcionite Redaction," *Annali di storia dell'esegesi* 29.1 (2012): 21–48; and Judith M. Lieu, *Marcion and the Making of a Heretic: God and Scripture in the Second Century* (Cambridge: Cambridge University Press, 2015), 196–209.

Marcion's *Gospel* are the most telling indications we have of the second major redactional layer of Luke.[55]

It could be that this major redaction of Luke, in concert with the creation of Acts, was directed against Marcion himself (as Tyson maintained), but it could also be that this redaction was aimed against Marcion's teacher, Cerdo, and/or a movement/community to which Marcion belonged and which he later represented during his teaching sojourn in Rome. That is to say, the later redaction of Luke need not be expressly anti-Marcionite in order to be opposed to the exclusive type of Paulinism that Marcion represented. Still, the anti-Marcionite redactions detailed by Tyson and Klinghardt have an analytical value for our analysis. They happen to be almost entirely identical to the significant portions of Luke that are otherwise inexplicably missing from the first edition of John. That is to say, Marcion's *Gospel* is a key witness to show us that the first edition of John did not depend on a singular, prior production of Luke-Acts, but instead on an early version of Luke.

Marcion's relevance extends not merely to Luke, but also to Acts and the second and third major editions of the

---

[55] Matthias Klinghardt, "The Marcionite Gospel and the Synoptic Problem: A New Suggestion," *NovT* 50.1 (2008): 1–27; Matthias Klinghardt, *Das älteste Evangelium und die Entstehung der kanonischen Evangelien* (2 vols.; TANZ 60; Tübingen: Francke, 2015); Matthias Klinghardt, "Marcion's Gospel and the New Testament: Catalyst or Consequence?" *NTS* 63.2 (2017): 318–23. See also Tyson, *Marcion and Luke-Acts*. In my view, Klinghardt's reconstruction of the Synoptic problem has a lot of merit, particularly in seeing early Luke (= Klinghardt's Marcionite *Gospel*) as influencing John, and final Luke as depending on John and Matthew, but it is unwarranted to postulate early Luke as preceding Mark and Matthew and influencing them. Thus Klinghardt's jettisoning of Q and the Two-Source Theory is unnecessary. Mimetic layers, particularly regarding Dionysus, are tremendously helpful in tracing out the Synoptic problem and its redactional layers. Early Luke's (= Marcion's) Dionysian imitations are novel developments not found in Mark or Matthew.

Gospel of John. For in all of these texts exclusive Paulinism is countered by the proto-Orthodox recovery of Peter and other original apostles. MacDonald rightly notes the dependence of John 21:3-11 on Luke 5:1-11, correctly ascribes this passage to the second redaction of John, and ably describes it as part of an extensive redactional effort to rehabilitate Peter.[56] Indeed, though MacDonald does not mention Marcion, MacDonald's extended sections on Peter and the Beloved Disciple as central characters in the second major edition of John are crucial to the case for reading this version of John as an involved redaction against the exclusive Paulinism that Marcion represented.[57] Canonical Luke and Acts follow suit, though they go to unforeseen lengths to recover Peter and valorize a primordial and continuous apostolic *collegium*. In my view, the second and third editions of John, the second edition of Luke, and Acts were all produced to counter the exclusive Paulinism represented (contemporaneously or later) by Marcion.

Pliny as a Redactional-Mimetic Pivot Point

Pliny the Younger—specifically, his trials and executions of Christians, his precedent-setting policy to refer Christian citizens to Rome, and his correspondence with Trajan, all taking place around 109-111 CE—is also a crucial pivot point between the early and later editions of both Luke and John. As Ilseo Park notes in his chapter below, citing Robert Grant and Courtney Friesen, Pliny's description of Christians "was shaped by Livy's account of Bacchanalia."[58]

---

[56] MacDonald, *Dionysian Gospel*, 139-40.

[57] MacDonald, *Dionysian Gospel*, 141-50 (Peter), 150-62 (Beloved Disciple).

[58] Ilseo Park, "Acts 2 as an Intertextual Map: Moving from Dionysian to Platonic Identity," *infra*. See Courtney J. P. Friesen, *Reading Dionysus: Euripides'* Bacchae *and the Cultural Contestations of Greeks, Jews,*

Given Pliny's prestige and imperial authority to set legal precedent as *legatus* of Bithynia-Pontus, this observation is far more consequential than mere literary characterization. Early Christians now suddenly faced official accusations of worshipping a Neos Dionysos and of engaging in *nova Bacchanalia* in violation of Trajan's rescript against *hetairia*. They had to answer, and answer they did.

As has been previously demonstrated, Acts knows Pliny's correspondence with Trajan and invents Paul's Roman citizenship so as to conform to Pliny's criteria for escaping execution and securing his Aenean passport to Rome, as it were.[59] Park's chapter below and his dissertation both amply demonstrate that Acts, while saturated with Dionysian imitations, frontloads these imitations and seeks to qualify, correct, and outdo them with Platonic/Socratic imitations. The emergence of Christianity according to Acts is the story of Socrates outdoing Dionysus, of Greek philosophy and Greek ritual correcting and taming Greek epic. Yet this is no mere literary plotline: it maps perfectly as an apologetic strategy answering to the historical, political, and legal dilemma that Christians faced after Pliny.

It also maps quite nicely against the redactional history of John and Luke.[60] The second redactional layer of John

---

Romans, and Christians (STAC 95; Tübingen: Mohr Siebeck, 2015), 22–23 and Robert M. Grant, "Pliny and the Christians," *HTR* 41.4 (1948): 273–74.

[59] Bilby, "Pliny's Correspondence" and Phillips, "How Did Paul Become a Roman 'Citizen'?" Both cited approvingly in Matthews, "Does Dating Luke-Acts into the Second Century Affect the Q Hypothesis?", 247.

[60] Here there is not room to explore in detail the geographical proximity and relationships among these texts. Suffice it to say that Marcion came from Pontus, a province governed by Pliny and then his successor Tertullus. Scholars typically locate the Johannine community in Asia Minor, and the production of Luke-Acts in the province of Asia. All that to say, the intertextuality described here is entirely concentrated in Asia Minor.

responds to Pliny by means of major additions and qualifications to its earlier, Dionysus-saturated vision: adding extended Socratic discourses, reconfiguring the passion as an *imitatio Socrati*, and stressing the tangibility of the resurrected body of Jesus.[61] The second redactional layer in Luke follows suit, though it evinces a far more rigorous tendency to evoke and simultaneously correct the Dionysian caricatures of the Christian founders. The same Bacchic-to-Socratic antetextual pattern that Ilseo Park identifies in Acts also obtains in the second redactional layer of Luke.[62] Its John the Baptist may still come from the wild and speak in oracles, but he ultimately belongs to a legitimate priestly lineage and proffers ethical/philosophical guidance to Roman tax collectors and soldiers (Luke 1:5-25, 57-80; 3:1-14). While the oracles and pregnancies of Elizabeth and Mary evoke Dionysian *ecstasis*, they are situated safely within the sanctioned context of imperial order, temple piety, and patrilineal heritage (Luke 1–3). Simeon may give an ecstatic oracle, but his speech is tempered by the concerns of an aged philosopher embracing his death (Luke 2:25–35).[63] Though divine in impetuous prerogative, the child Jesus exemplifies festival and temple piety, Socratic dialogue with Jerusalem's teachers, and filial piety to God and parents (Luke 2:41–52). The "bodily" dove in Luke effectively transforms the giving of the Spirit from an ecstatic experience to a sanctioned omen (Luke 3:22). In the Lukan passion (Luke 23), the character of Jesus transforms

---

[61] The Socratic tendency in the second edition of John may nuance MacDonald's Dionysian parallels at points. For example, in John 18:19-21, while the opening theme of interrogation may be either Dionysian or Socratic/philosophical, the self-defense of Jesus as one who has "spoken boldly in the world; often taught in the synagogue and in the temple" in 18:20-21 better fits a later counter-Plinian redaction that characterizes Jesus as a noble philosopher.

[62] Park, "Acts 2 as an Intertextual Map," *infra*.

[63] See n. 64 below about the depiction of Seneca in Tacitus.

into a new Socrates, and his women followers who verge on Dionysian excess in their mourning remain pious and focus on their funerary ritual duties (Luke 23:27ff). The final layer of Luke follows and outdoes the Dionysian correctives in the second and third layer of John by placing an even greater stress on the capacity of the body of the resurrected Jesus to eat and to be touched (Luke 24:37–43), as well as by its insistence that the holy spirit was not imparted directly by Jesus, but instead was to come as a later omen tied to a sanctioned Jewish religious festival in the capital city, an event anticipated with devout temple ritual (Luke 24:49–52).

These counter-Marcionite (or counter-proto-Marcionite) and counter-Plinian redactions dovetail.[64] The same Lukan passages and phrases that run against the Dionysian grain are all also absent from Marcion's *Gospel*. They also have a retrospective value in explaining just why Marcion's later detractors were given to accuse him falsely of denying the bodily resurrection of Jesus. Marcion included references to the resurrection of the body of Jesus both in his *Evangelion* and his *Apostolikon* (which included 1 Cor 15). But he also preserved intact earlier Dionysian motifs of Jesus escaping arrest and even death by becoming invisible and intangible, and his early version of Luke did not have quite so strong of an emphasis on the post-resurrection body of Jesus. The discrepancies between Marcion's early Luke and the canonical/proto-Orthodox Luke led to Marcion's detractors accusing him of docetism and exaggerating their case. What

---

[64] Gregory E. Sterling, "*Mors philosophi*: The Death of Jesus in Luke," *HTR* 94.4 (2001): 383–402. Of special note here is Sterling's observation that Pliny is the earliest Latin author to attest to the genre of the *exitus illustrium virorum* ("*Mors philosophi*," 386). Pliny's subject matter in this regard pertained to the death of Stoic philosophers under Nero and Domitian. Sterling also notes that Tacitus followed this genre in his description of the aged Seneca as an *imitatio Socrati* ("*Mors philosophi*," 389–90).

their criticisms actually highlight is the tendency of the redactors of John and Luke to insert increasingly vivid descriptions of the resurrected body of Jesus as part of their counter-Dionysian response to Pliny.

Mapping Mimetic-Redactional Layers

In summary, I fully agree with MacDonald that the first edition of John deserves to be called *the* Dionysian Gospel and that it often relies on Luke. What I have attempted to do is to nuance, correct, and further MacDonald's work by bringing it into conversation with redaction-critical scholarship on Luke as well as with recent scholarship on Marcion and Pliny the Younger. This goes together with my new assessment of the compositional, redactional, and mimetic history of the Gospels and Acts.

- Early/Shorter Mark (ca. 70–80) thoroughly imitated Homer's *Iliad* and *Odyssey*;
- Matthew (ca. 80–100) used Q and Mark, borrowing Mark's imitations of Homer, and adding imitations of Plutarch (*Vita Alexandri*);
- First Edition of Luke (ca. 80–100) used Q and Mark, borrowing Mark's imitations of Homer, and added emulations of the *Bacchae* (Luke 4:29–30; 5:1–11; 8:1–3; 19:1–2, 8–10) which were later attested by Marcion;
- First Edition of John (ca. 100–111) used Mark (including its imitations of Homer) and Luke (including its Dionysian content, e.g., Luke 4:29–30 inspired John 8:58b–59 and 10:39), but developed its own focused, thoroughgoing imitation of the *Bacchae* of Euripides;
- Second and Third Edition of John (ca. 112–138) qualified its earlier Dionysian imitations by adding new imitations of Plato (Socrates);
- Second Edition of Luke (ca. 117–150), inspired by the second and/or third edition of John and using

Matthew, added new imitations of Euripides, Homer, Josephus, Livy, Plato (Socrates), Plutarch, Suetonius, Vergil, and Xenophon, all of which are not present or unattested in Marcion and all of which lack clear parallels in John;
- Acts, created jointly with the Second Edition of Luke (ca. 117–150) and inspired by the second and/or third edition of John, developed new imitations of Aeschylus, Euripides, Homer, Josephus, Pindar, Plato (Socrates), Vergil, and Xenophon.

One wonders whether the Jesus-Dionysus program of the original Gospel of John actually contributed to Christians being accused of Bacchanalian crimes by mobs in Asia Minor, ultimately bringing them to Pliny's attention. In any case, Pliny changed things, historically and literarily. He made it indefensible for Christians afterward to pair Jesus and Dionysus without a very healthy amount of learned philosophy, pious ritual, and careful deference to Roman authority.

Pliny's dealings with Christians supplies the decisive *terminus ante quem* for the Dionysian Gospel. In view of Pliny's trials and the publication of his correspondence around 109–111 CE, the first edition of the Gospel of John does not date to 117 CE as MacDonald stated, but instead to 111 CE at the latest. Even in terms of a cushion for transmission and influence, it seems highly unlikely that Luke-Acts was quickly produced in a single go around 115 CE, just barely in time for the first edition of John to appropriate it around 117 CE. Like the Gospel of John, the Gospel of Luke was composed in stages, and the influence between these compositional projects traveled more slowly and in both directions.

In sum, the first edition of John depended on the first edition of Luke and took inspiration from its few Dionysian episodes to craft a full-fledged Dionysian Gospel. After Pliny and the emergence of a proto-Marcionite or Marcionite exclusive Paulinism, the second and third editions of John radically tempered this Dionysian vision with a Socratic vision and diligently recovered the character of Peter and at least one other early apostle. That re-envisioning inspired the second layer of Luke and Acts to undertake a far more ambitious endeavor, both in terms of a rigorous and eclectic mimesis of classical sources and in terms of molding a proto-Orthodox account of primal apostolic unity and complementarity between the earliest apostles and Paul.

As MacDonald himself has repeatedly shown, creative, critical, and even subversive imitations are often the most sincere. So let us set aside the notion that imitation is the sincerest form of flattery only if it is slavish. At the same time, let us also give ample credit where credit is due, credit to Dennis MacDonald for brilliantly pioneering and resourcing an entire school of Biblical interpretation in mimesis criticism, credit to the author of the Dionysian Gospel for pioneering the first major Christian imitation of the *Bacchae* of Euripides, and credit to the later editors of John and Luke-Acts for appropriating yet radically qualifying this Dionysian vision. As MacDonald himself has conclusively demonstrated, the early Gospel of John is *the* Dionysian Gospel.

It was not canonical Luke and Acts that inspired the Dionysian Gospel, but instead early Luke (essentially Marcion's *Gospel*). MacDonald is right that the second and third editions of John sought to qualify this Dionysian vision with a Socratic one. Yet contemporaneous historical events/currents must also inform our literary reconstructions: namely, the pivotal roles of Pliny's execution of Christians for Bacchanalian crimes and the emergence of a Marcionite (or proto-Marcionite) exclusive Paulinism. The second and third editions of John responded to these currents by recasting Jesus as a new Socrates and by recovering Peter in the interest of proto-Orthodoxy. Taking inspiration from a later edition of

John, the second/canonical edition of Luke, together with Acts, expands, corrects, and nuances this Socrates-bests-Dionysus proto-Orthodox program, yet to a far greater extent and as part of a far more ranging and learned mimetic project. Ironically, the expansive and eclectic mimetic undertaking in Luke and Acts provides some of the strongest evidence we have against the first edition of John depending on the canonical edition of Luke.

Mimesis in Practice
Discovering Old Imitations Anew

Scriptural Revision in Mark's Gospel and Philostratus's Life of Apollonius
Austin Busch

Broadening Mimesis from Biblical Interpretation to Classical Reception

In one Markan episode after another, Dennis MacDonald follows traces of Homer in a careful and sometimes creative attempt to discern how the evangelist remakes heroic epic into Gospel.[1] In this essay I explore MacDonald's reading of Mark with reference to a specific pattern of Homeric allusions that he discovers, namely a configuration of transformative allusions to the Cyclopeia — Odysseus's battle with the Cyclops Polyphemus in book 9 of the *Odyssey*. I situate that allusive complex within a theologically coherent interpretation of Jesus's death and resurrection in Mark's Gospel before comparing it to a similar configuration in an analogous ancient literary work, Philostratus's *Life of Apollonius*. The *Life of Apollonius*, I argue, resembles Mark's Gospel both in its overarching project of Homeric transformation and in its deployment and interpretive development of the Polyphemus episode in particular.

---

[1] I am grateful to Dennis MacDonald for his response to a version of this paper read during a session of the Bible, Myth, and Myth Theory program unit at the 2015 SBL annual meeting, as well as anonymous members of the audience whose comments and critiques I found immensely helpful. I also thank Amy Lauricella for her invaluable assistance with research.

This fact should be brought to bear on the problem of the *Life's* literary relationship to the canonical Gospels, which demands more sustained attention than it has received. I do not attempt to resolve that particular problem here, but I do probe its dimensions and pursue its implications in order to show how it relates to a number of broader questions toward which MacDonald's work often gestures, even if MacDonald does not address them in a sustained way: What are the broad contours not of earliest "Christian" Biblical interpretation, but rather of ancient Mediterranean scriptural interpretation? What strategies, tactics, and rhetorical moves do interpreters of canonically authoritative texts, including but not limited to the Bible, employ in the Roman imperial world? How might we understand ancient interpretations of Homer and of the Bible as part of a single phenomenon involving individual and communities of readers confronting claims made on the intellect and on the imagination by supremely authoritative literary corpora, that is, by writings habitually invoked to resolve questions of cultural identity, of moral behavior, and of religious truth? This problem is more discrete than that of "literary interpretation," but broader than "Biblical interpretation," and when it is articulated in terms such as the above, it suggests that much of what appears idiosyncratic about Markan and Philostratean scriptural interpretation—including some of the more controversial discoveries MacDonald claims to make—is actually quite conventional.

Mark's Imitation of the Cyclopeia

MacDonald persuasively argues that Mark on two separate occasions refers to the Cyclopeia, perhaps the most famous myth of a hero's battle with a monster in classical antiquity.[2] As MacDonald observes, Jesus's victory over the

---

[2] See Dennis R. MacDonald, *The Homeric Epics and the Gospel of Mark* (New Haven: Yale University Press, 2000), 67–76 and Dennis R.

demonic Legion in Mark 5 seems modeled on the Homeric episode. Below I summarize some of the most significant parallels he observes in his writings on this Markan scene, which I supplement with insights and analysis of my own.

(1) In both stories, a sea voyage brings the hero and his companions into the proximity of a monstrous savage (*Od.* 9.105-07; Mark 5:1), whose violent unsociability is figured in his dwelling not in humane community, but rather in caverns (ἐν σπέσσι, *Od.* 9.114, 182, etc.; ἐν τοῖς μνήμασιν ["tombs"] in Mark 5:2, 3, etc., to be understood as caverns, as indicated by the reference in 15:46 to Jesus's burial ἐν μνημείῳ ὃ ἦν λελατομημένον ἐκ πέτρας ["in a tomb that had been hewn out of rock"]).³

(2) In both stories, the monstrous savage has herdsmen for neighbors who fail to help him and who bear witness to their inability to challenge the heroic invader's disturbance of their territory.⁴ The other Cyclopes, falling for Odysseus's ruse, conclude that Zeus must be responsible for Polyphemus's ailment and that there is nothing they can do for him (*Od.* 9.399-412).⁵ The Gerasenes initially fail to assist

---

MacDonald, *The Gospels and Homer: Imitations of Greek Epic in Mark and Luke-Acts* (NTGL 1; Lanham, MD: Rowman & Littlefield, 2015), 199-204, 213-21.

³ See MacDonald, *Homeric Epics*, 67-69 and MacDonald, *Gospels and Homer*, 214. I quote NA[28] and Thomas W. Allen, ed., *Homeri Opera* (2nd ed.; OCT; Oxford: Clarendon, 1917). Unless otherwise noted, translations of ancient texts are my own.

⁴ See MacDonald, *Homeric Epics*, 71 and MacDonald, *Gospels and Homer*, 217.

⁵ If the Cyclopes are implying that Polyphemus is going mad—a standard interpretation of νοῦσον . . . Διὸς μεγάλου ἀλέασθαι (9.411; cf. W. Walter Merry et al., *Homer's* Odyssey, 2 vols. [Oxford: Clarendon, 1886-1901], 1:387; and compare the reference to divinely inspired madness at Sophocles, *Aj.* 185: ἥκοι γὰρ ἂν θεία νόσος)—then the parallel with Mark is even stronger. Neither Polyphemus's fellow Cyclopes nor the Gerasenes

the demoniac (Mark 5:3-4); later, prompted by their swineherds, they actively beg Jesus to depart after his actions lead to the destruction of their herds (5:14-17).

(3) In both stories, the hero's defeat of the monster involves a treacherously ambiguous moment of naming.[6] Odysseus famously identifies himself as Οὖτις, "Nobody" (9.366-67), thereby undermining Polyphemus's cry for help from his herdsman neighbors: ὦ φίλοι, Οὖτίς με κτείνει δόλῳ οὐδὲ βίηφιν (9.408). Homer's name play involves a grammatical anomaly. Although Polyphemus understands οὖτις as a proper name, he says not Οὖτίς με κτείνει δόλῳ καὶ βίηφιν, but rather οὖτίς με δόλῳ <u>οὐδὲ</u> βίηφιν, with οὐδὲ picking up on οὖτις as a negative pronoun, rather than a homonymic proper noun. To capture the effect in English, Polyphemus might say, "nobody harms me by treachery nor by violence," instead of "Nobody harms me by treachery and violence." In any case, the inconsistency makes plausible the neighboring Cyclopes's misunderstanding of Polyphemus's declaration, while at the same time reflecting the befuddlement of this particular Cyclops's intellect: regardless of what he means to say, since Polyphemus begins with οὖτις, his tongue carries him mindlessly through the sentence as if he actually meant to employ the word according to normal usage, as a negative indefinite pronoun, rather than as the identically sounding name Odysseus has given him.[7]

---

are able to assist the one whom they imagine insane as a result of divine or demonic manipulation (cf. Mark 5:15).

[6] See MacDonald, *Homeric Epics*, 69-70 and MacDonald *Gospels and Homer*, 216.

[7] For another interpretive possibility, see Merry et al., *Homer's Odyssey*, 1:387: "Polyphemus intended to signify, 'he is slaying me by craft, *and not* by violence.'" Seth L. Schein integrates this interpretation into his very interesting reading of the scene ("Odysseus and Polyphemus in the *Odyssey*," *GRBS* 11.2 [1970]: 73-83, here 79-80). See Herbert Weir Smyth, *Greek Grammar* (rev. Gordon M. Messing; Cambridge, MA: Harvard

In Mark 5, the demons, presumably in an attempt to evade the power Jesus would have over them were he to learn their names, ambiguously respond to his inquiry about their identity with the vague moniker "Legion": λεγιὼν ὄνομά μοι, ὅτι πολλοί ἐσμεν ("my name is Legion, because we are many"; 5:9).[8] This passage also displays a grammatical irregularity: the first-person singular pronoun μοι ("my") gives way to a first-person plural verb ἐσμεν ("we are"), creating a miniature anacoluthon. This irregularity too is most expeditiously interpreted as a product of the demoniac's befuddlement — the proliferation and confusion of identities in a man possessed by multiple unclean spirits.[9]

(4) In both stories, the hero's defeat of the monster relies on a trick involving livestock that complements the deceptive naming. After Odysseus blinds the Cyclops in his drunken sleep, Polyphemus blocks the entrance to the cave, but he is forced to allow his bleating sheep out to pasture and carefully inspects the exiting flock for human contraband by feeling their backs with his hands. Odysseus has hidden his men under the sheep's bellies, so that they evade his

---

University Press, 1956) and compare Smyth, *Greek Grammar*, 2939 (my reading) with Smyth, *Greek Grammar*, 2934 (the alternative approach). While the alternative interpretation of Polyphemus's words makes good sense of them as a response to the other Cyclopes' question (ἦ μή τίς σ' αὐτὸν κτείνει δόλῳ ἠὲ βίηφιν; 406), the idea that the monster would mean flatly to deny Odysseus's violence seems difficult to square with the fact that the hero has just put his eye out.

[8] Julius Wellhausen, *Das Evangelium Marci übersetzt und erklärt* (2nd ed.; Berlin: Reimer, 1903), 39 and Campbell Bonner, "The Technique of Exorcism," *HTR* 36.1 (1943): 39–49, here 44.

[9] See Robert H. Gundry, *Mark: A Commentary on His Apology for the Cross* (Grand Rapids: Eerdmans, 1993), 261 for a careful attempt to sort out this grammatical confusion, which actually serves to show how intricately the demoniac's confusion of identities is woven into the fabric of Mark's narrative. One finds similar grammatical confusion in other stories of demonic possession in Mark (e.g., 1:24).

inspection and escape (*Od.* 9.413-63). Analogously, the Markan demons, in an attempt to avoid expulsion from the land, request to be allowed entrance into a herd of swine that nearby herdsmen are shepherding (5:10-12).[10] Jesus grants their wish, but their plan of escape fails, for instead of sheltering the demons, the pigs immediately rush into the sea and drown (5:13).[11]

---

[10] Though MacDonald observes this parallel, it is not entirely clear what he makes of it, and he seems more interested in connecting it with the Circe episode in *Od.* 10.135-465 than in interpreting it within the context of Mark's engagement with the Cyclopeia. See MacDonald, *Homeric Epics*, 70 and MacDonald, *Gospels and Homer*, 216-17.

[11] Readers since antiquity have struggled to understand the sudden introduction of these swine into the story, as well as the pigs' equally surprising destruction after Jesus seemingly allows the demons the reprieve of entrance into them. The discussion of this passage in Macarius Magnes, *Apocr.* 3.4 testifies to the widespread and early confusion it occasioned. Modern commentators have offered a variety of solutions to its problems. R. H. Lightfoot argued that Jesus cleanses the Gentile land of unclean beasts, as he does the man of unclean spirits (*History and Interpretation in the Gospels* [New York: Harper, 1934], 89-90). Joel Marcus plays up the episode's political connotations, likening the horde of demons to an invading army, such as Pharaoh's, which is drowned because of an "incapability of restraining ... brutal rage" that leads it to destroy the very lodgings it attempts to control, thereby thwarting its desire to remain in the land it occupies (*Mark 1-16: A New Translation with Introduction and Commentary* [2 vols.; AB 27-27A; New York: Doubleday; New Haven: Yale University Press, 2000-2009], 1:352; cf. Rikki E. Watts, *Isaiah's New Exodus in Mark*, WUNT II/88 [Tübingen: Mohr Siebeck, 1997], 160). Adela Yarbro Collins speculates that the story is related to various ancient traditions of illness transferred to animals (*Mark: A Commentary* [ed. Harold W. Attridge; Hermeneia; Minneapolis: Fortress, 2007], 270). Of course, other explanations of the narrative oddity have been offered (e.g., that the destruction of many swine testifies to Jesus's extraordinary exorcism of not one but a horde of demons, an interpretation which would seem to go back at least to Jerome, *Vit. Hil.* 23), and such explanations are not mutually exclusive. However, the sudden introduction of the herd of livestock here, as well as their peculiar demise, is quite efficiently accounted for by positing that Mark's narrative, in this section at least, does not so much

An intriguing transposition emerges from these parallels. Mark's demons attempt to avoid defeat at Jesus's hands by employing treacherous tactics analogous to those Odysseus uses on Polyphemus, which include the hero identifying himself with a false and ambiguous name, and his seeking of safety for himself and his men by hiding among livestock. Thus does Mark displace underhanded deception from the Homeric hero onto his story's monster, and ensure that it fails rather than succeeds.[12] The demons' nominal evasion is useless in limiting Jesus's power over them, as is their negotiation with him to enter the swine. Although this initial interpretive inference must be complicated, it does seem that Mark cleanses the Cyclopeia of the most morally dubious heroic deception, much as Jesus purifies the man of unclean spirits and the territory he visits of impure animals.

Even in the midst of this careful refinement, however, Mark's Jesus arguably still shows himself to be a subdued sort of Odyssean trickster. In granting the demons' request to enter the swine in order that they might remain in the land, Jesus ensures their destruction even as he allows them to stay, for the nearby pigs, presumably shocked and tormented by their sudden demonic possession, promptly commit suicide. While Jesus does not actively deceive the demons, he does facilitate their self-deception by allowing them to imagine they have successfully negotiated with "the son of the most high God" in order to limit the scope of the expulsion he orders (5:7). As I shall argue below, the demonic forces mistakenly imagine they can negotiate another deal with Jesus later on in Mark, at which point Jesus again encourages their erroneous belief that they have the upper hand.

---

generate its own narrative logic as adapt and revise interrelated Homeric motifs in a thematically strategic manner.

[12] See MacDonald, *Homeric Epics*, 74.

(5) Both stories close on a similar note. Once the monster is defeated and Odysseus is safe on his ship, Homer's hero proclaims his real name, foolishly boasting so that the monster knows just who vanquished him (9.502–05) and thereby allowing Polyphemus to curse him effectively (9.526–36). Complementarily, just before embarking, Mark's Jesus eschews his well-known penchant for secrecy and orders the man from whom he had just driven out the demons to tell his friends ὅσα ὁ κύριός σοι πεποίηκεν ("how much the Lord has done for you"; Mark 5:19). The man actually ἤρξατο κηρύσσειν ἐν τῇ Δεκαπόλει ὅσα ἐποίησεν αὐτῷ ὁ Ἰησοῦς, καὶ πάντες ἐθαύμαζον ("began to proclaim in the Decapolis how much Jesus did for him, and all were amazed"; 5:20). Jesus does not grasp after glory in Mark, as Odysseus does in Homer, but he receives it nonetheless.[13] Once again, Mark's adaptation of Homer tends toward reducing or redeeming problematic traits the Homeric hero displays.

(6) Mark 5 is quite closely related to Mark 16, where the hero Jesus once again confronts an evil entity associated with cavernous tombs and thereby likened to Polyphemus. In chapter 5, the horde of demons orchestrates its victim's social destruction, ensuring his communal alienation by settling him among the dead. In Mark 16, death is literal, its power ensuring that Jesus is shut within a tomb. This is the problem the women coming to anoint Jesus's decomposing body acknowledge when they approach and ask τίς ἀποκυλίσει ἡμῖν τὸν λίθον ἐκ τῆς θύρας τοῦ μνημείου; ("Who will roll away for us the stone from the entrance of the tomb?"; 16:3). As MacDonald nicely observes, this is the very problem Odysseus and his men face in *Od.* 9, when the monster Polyphemus traps them in a cave by rolling in front of it a great stone they are incapable of removing on their own,

---

[13] See MacDonald, *Homeric Epics*, 72 and MacDonald, *Gospels and Homer*, 216.

before he begins to kill and eat them (*Od.* 9.240–43).¹⁴ In the *Odyssey*, as discussed above, the hero escapes from the unseeing Cyclops's cave by treacherously blinding Polyphemus and then hiding under the sheep when the monster opens the cave to let them out to pasture. In Mark, the removal of the stone and opening of Jesus's tomb is a mystery that is never resolved (16:4), but the result is much the same: as Odysseus and his men escape the monster Polyphemus's deadly clutches, so is Jesus liberated from the power of death—as are his followers, when one considers that the earliest believers understood Jesus's resurrection as the "first fruits" of a general resurrection of the dead (1 Cor 15:20–23; cf. Matt 27:53).¹⁵

Polyphemus in Mark's Gospel and Virgil's *Aeneid*

These interrelated Homeric echoes make a great deal of sense in the Markan thematic context in which they are deployed. There was probably no monster in classical antiquity more famous than Polyphemus. This anthropophagic one-eyed savage was such a well-known

---

¹⁴ See MacDonald, *Homeric Epics*, 74–76 and MacDonald, *Gospels and Homer*, 200–04.

¹⁵ From very early in the Christian literary tradition, scribes have recognized and sought to amplify subtle allusions to the Polyphemus scene in Mark's innovative account of Jesus's empty tomb. As MacDonald notes in *Gospels and Homer*, 201–03, a variant reading of Luke 23:53, itself a revision of Mark 15:46's initial reference to Jesus's cavernous tomb and the stone rolled in front of it, assimilates this stone to the one guarding Polyphemus's cave by describing it with the relative clause ὃν μόγις εἴκοσι ἐλύλιον (see discussion in Bruce M. Metzger, *A Textual Commentary on the Greek New Testament* [2nd ed.; Stuttgart: Deutsche Bibelgesellschaft, 1994], 156). The phrase echoes and simplifies Homer's claim that οὐκ ἂν τόν γε δύω καὶ εἴκοσ' ἄμαξαι / ἐσθλαὶ τετράκυκλοι ἀπ' οὔδεος ὀχλίσσειαν (9.240–41). Recension 2 of the Byzantine Homeric *Centos* use the same Homeric lines to describe the stone rolled in front of Jesus's tomb (1.2092–94), as MacDonald also observes (*Gospels and Homer*, 203–04).

terror that in the Hellenistic period he becomes the subject of satire: Theocritus cleverly elaborates an alternative mythical tradition to represent him as the violently buffoonish suitor of the beautiful nymph Galatea (*Id.* 6 and 11). Despite the parodic development, however, Polyphemus remains a horrible and ghastly figure in the imperial era. Vergil deploys him with especially eerie effectiveness at the end of *Aen.* 3, when Aeneas and his crew rescue Achaemenides, a man Odysseus had left behind on Sicily (the supposed location of the events of *Od.* 9). Vergil's description of Polyphemus's violence is gruesome in the extreme—darker and more disturbing than Homer's account (compare *Od.* 9.288-93 and *Aen.* 3.621-27).[16] Moreover, after departing, Aeneas and his men hear Polyphemus's terrifying roar and turn back to see a *concilium horrendum* ("dreadful assembly"), the community of Cyclopes having rushed from woods and mountains to the beach, reaching with their heads to the sky like the tallest of trees, their lone eyes scowling (*Aen.* 3.675-81).[17]

Vergil at this point links Polyphemus and his companions to the underworld, for a *clamorem immensum* ("boundless cry") bellows from within Aetna's caves, shakes the waves of the sea, and is felt as far away as Italy (*Aen.* 3.672-74). The narrative development mythologizes seismic activity associated the Sicilian volcano Mount Aetna by attributing it to Polyphemus and his companions. Polyphemus thereby becomes more than merely another monster Aeneas encounters in his journey to Italy; he is a forerunner of the horrifying chthonic deities that surface with progressive frequency in the second half of the *Aeneid*, as

---

[16] As recognized by Justin Glenn, even in his sensitive attempt to do justice to the pathetic elements of the Cyclops's Virgilian characterization ("Virgil's Polyphemus," *GR* 19.1 [1972]: 47-59, here 58).

[17] I quote R. A. B. Mynors, ed., *P. Vergili Maronis Opera* (OCT; Oxford: Clarendon, 1969).

Vergil's epic deposits its hero in a world that becomes, if possible for a survivor of the Trojan War, increasingly violent and grim.[18] These monsters include the cave-dwelling Cacus, who decorates his home with the heads and entrails of his human victims and, like Polyphemus, is associated with seismic activity (10.185–307). Also included are the ghastly furies Tisiphone (6.570–72), Allecto (7.323–551), and Megaera, the last represented by her twin daughters the *dirae* (12.845–86).[19] Although not a monster *per se*, Mezentius too should be added to the list (8.481–93).[20] In this context, Aeneas's escape with all of his people from Polyphemus, the first in a parade of increasingly terrifying chthonic monsters the *Aeneid* features—and with a man Odysseus had unwittingly left behind in his own fearful flight—signals the heroic superiority of Vergil's hero to Homer's Odysseus.

Mark's allusive integration of the Cyclopeia leverages the same emotional and emulative power as Vergil's. On the one hand, it colors the weird and disturbing scene the evangelist paints in his vivid account of Jesus's confrontation with the demoniac; on the other, it emphasizes the heroic magnitude of Jesus's defeat of the demonic horde who had kept its victim chained among tombs. Even more significantly, it foreshadows and underscores the significance of Jesus's

---

[18] Compare Brooks Otis's interpretation of the scene in *Virgil: A Study in Civilized Poetry* (Oxford: Clarendon, 1964), 262–64, which views Achaemenides as a figure of Aeneas. Soon to be bereft of Anchises, he will likewise be "left alone in a world of *monstra*" (264).

[19] Although the *dirae* serve at the throne of Jupiter, they are offspring of Megaera, one of the two furies that Virgil locates with their sister Tisiphone in the underworld (6.570–72).

[20] Classicists have frequently noted parallels between Polyphemus and these figures. See, for instance, Justin Glenn, "Mezentius and Polyphemus," *AJP* 92.2 (1971): 129–55; Howard Jacobson, "Cacus and the Cyclops," *Mnemosyne* 42.1 (1989): 101–02; and David Sansone, "Cacus and the Cyclops: An Addendum" *Mnemosyne* 44.1 (1991): 171.

final salvific task—his miraculous liberation from death itself, which temporarily locks him within a cavernous tomb (Mark 15:45-46), as Polyphemus does Odysseus.

The Centrality of the Cyclopeia in the Narrative Theology of Mark

Mark's specific employment of the Cylopeia is an important element of his strategic representation of Jesus's ministry, death, and resurrection as a vanquishment of demonic forces. After his initiation through baptism, Jesus's ministry begins in direct confrontation with Satan (Mark 1:12-13), and then immediately spills into one account of demonic exorcism after another (1:21-28, 34; 3:11; 5:1-20; 6:7, 24-30; 9:14-29; etc.). A scribal dispute about Jesus's exorcistic powers leads Jesus to reflect on his ministry in chapter 3 (vv. 22-30), where he describes it in parables as the binding of demons and the liberation of people from their clutches (3:27). Several chapters later Jesus articulates a slightly altered vision of his mission: instead of violently overcoming hostile demonic forces in order to free individual people from them, Jesus will give his life to these forces as a ransom in return for the manumission of many enslaved (10:45).[21]

Understanding Jesus's death in this light more satisfactorily explains the centurion's exclamation upon seeing Jesus die than does tendentious insistence that his words constitute a something approaching a Christian confession: ἀληθῶς οὗτος ὁ ἄνθρωπος υἱὸς θεοῦ ἦν ("truly this man was son of God"; 15:39). Although his sentence echoes earlier declarations God makes in Mark (1:11; 9:7), it resembles those of demons no less closely (cf. 1:24), especially that of Legion (Ἰησοῦ υἱὲ τοῦ θεοῦ τοῦ ὑψίστου ["Jesus, Son of the most high

---

[21] For an important statement of this interpretation of Mark's theology of the atonement, see Anton Fridrichsen, "The Conflict of Jesus with the Unclean Spirits," *Theology* 22.129 (1931): 122-35.

God"]; 5:7),[22] and it would seem to make more sense in the context of Mark's overarching narrative to assimilate the voice of the Roman officer overseeing Jesus's unjust death to a demon possessing that man rather than to God.[23] This is

---

[22] The allusion is even stronger than it appears. As Whitney T. Shiner observes in "The Ambiguous Pronouncement of the Centurion and the Shrouding of Meaning in Mark," *JSNT* 22.78 (2000): 3-22: "Mark uses 'the Son of God' or a closely equivalent phrase several times in his Gospel. Every time that such phrases appear as predicate nominatives, Mark uses the article (1.11; 3.11; 9.7; 14.61). The article also appears when a demon identifies Jesus as 'the Holy One of God' (1.24) and when 'the Son' is used alone as a title (13.32). In contrast, there are only two times [other than 15:39] when the article is omitted before υἱός used as a title. In both these cases υἱός appears as an appositive to the name Jesus or Jesus Messiah (1.1; 5.7)" (6). One must add, however, that the use of υἱὸς θεοῦ in 1:1 is textually suspect (see Collins, *Mark*, 130 and the works there cited). Thus, the unusual lack of the article with the distinctive moniker υἱὸς θεοῦ in 15:39 and 5:7 alone increases the likelihood that 15:39 recalls 5:7 in particular.

[23] I here simplify and dichotomize a range of interpretive options for dealing with Mark 15:39, which Collins, for instance, treats more fully in her commentary (*Mark*, 764-71). And, of course, the atonement has a "double aspect," as Gustaf Aulén has argued, so that Christ's life given as a ransom to the demonic powers is necessarily and simultaneously a sacrifice that satisfies God's wrath (*Christus Victor: An Historical Study of the Three Main Types of the Idea of the Atonement*, trans. A. G. Herbert [New York: Macmillan, 1969], 55-60). Mark himself acknowledges this (14:23-24, 36). But granting the stipulation, much commentary on 15:39 basically assimilates it to its Matthean and Lukan revisions, each of which alter Mark in order to make the centurion's confession straightforwardly positive. Gundry, for instance, drawing on Howard M. Jackson, "The Death of Jesus in Mark and the Miracle from the Cross," *NTS* 33.1 (1987), 16-37, presumes that the centurion's declaration is predicated on the fact that he saw "the Wind of the Spirit, exhaled when in his last breath Jesus let loose a loud shout, ren[d] that veil [of the temple] in two from top to bottom. The veil-rending has not interrupted the two references in vv. 37, 39 to Jesus's expiration, then, so much as it has detailed the visible effect of his expiration (thus we should interpret the paratactic καί, 'and,' at the start of v. 38 as ecbatic: 'with the result that') and thereby told what the

especially the case when one recognizes the semantic connection between the demon identified as λεγιών and the Roman soldier identified as a κεντυρίων. Both terms are transliterations into Greek of Latin words referring to Roman soldiers: *Legio* refers to a division of the Roman army consisting of several thousand soldiers; *centurio* is the equivalent of a high ranking noncommissioned officer within that army. By having these two analogously named characters utter virtually the same words about Jesus (compare 5:6 and 15:39), Mark suggests that the Roman centurion is no less demonic than was Legion.[24] Such a suggestion would not have been particularly controversial among Mark's earliest readers: Mark was not the only New Testament author to suggest a connection between Roman political or military power and demonic forces, and a strong exegetical case may be made that the Second Evangelist, much like the author of

---

centurion saw that evoked his declaration" (*Mark*, 950). It is hard to imagine how a reader of Mark without access to Matthew's revision of this passage, which specifies that this centurion saw τὸν σεισμὸν καὶ τὰ γενόμενα ἐφοβήθησαν σφόδρα immediately before declaring Jesus was "son of God" (27:54), could draw the conclusion that the centurion in Mark, who stands facing Jesus and makes his confession after seeing him die with a loud cry (15:37, 39), actually has in mind the rending of the temple curtain, of which the Second Evangelist never even claims the centurion is even aware. (Gundry seems to recognize this problem later in his commentary [*Mark*, 970].) Without such tendentious presumptions, and with the possible echo of the demons in 5:7 especially, it makes more sense to presume that the centurion's declaration represents the same opposition to Jesus found in the cries of the demons Jesus confronts, than it does to shoe-horn it into a proto-Christian confession of the divinity of the crucified Christ.

[24] Much has been written about possible anti-Roman political implications of the Legion pericope. Most recently, see Warren Carter, "Cross-Gendered Romans and Mark's Jesus: Legion Enters the Pigs (Mark 5:1–20)," *JBL* 134.1 (2015): 139–55. In light of this research, it seems hard to deny that there is at the very least a "political nuance" to it (see Marcus, *Mark*, 1:351–52).

Revelation, understands the monsters from the vision in Dan 7 as demonic entities sponsoring Rome.[25]

Mark, then, presents an overarching narrative of Jesus's ministry according to which Jesus begins by freeing individual victims from demonic forces by means of discrete violent confrontations (3:27). Later he determines to give himself as a ransom to those forces in order to free many victims all at once (10:45). At the behest of his father, he delivers himself on the cross to the demons, who possess or otherwise control the Roman military commander overseeing his crucifixion.[26] They momentarily acquire authority over Jesus under the auspices of death, which is itself perhaps understood by Mark, like Paul, as a hypostasized spiritual power.[27] Their impending agency over Jesus would explain

---

[25] In Mark 13:14, just before echoing Dan 12:2's prophesy of tribulation preceding resurrection (Mark 13:19), Mark invokes Daniel's vague description of Antiochus's sacrilege (Dan 9:26-27) as a coded statement about Roman forces' defilement and destruction of the temple in 70 CE (Mark 13:2). (See Brian J. Incigneri, *The Gospel to the Romans: The Setting and Rhetoric of Mark's Gospel* [BibInt 65; Leiden: Brill, 2003], 126-33, especially 130-33). While scholars today recognize that the fourth beast in Dan 7 represents Syria and the king figured by its eleventh horn Antiochus IV Epiphanes (7:24-25, cf. v. 8), whose oppressive and sacrilegious behavior is imaginatively represented throughout the book (e.g. 8:9-14; 9:26-27, the passage Mark invokes in 13:19), early Christian interpreters tended to understand Daniel's fourth beast as Rome and/or its demonic sponsor and its horn as a Roman ruler (compare Dan 7 and Rev 13:1-9).

[26] Although I understand Jesus's conflict with demons on the cross very differently, see the perceptive analysis of Frederick W. Danker, "The Demonic Secret in Mark: A Reexamination of the Cry of Dereliction (15.34)," *ZNW* 61.1-2 (1970): 48-69.

[27] Cf. 1 Cor 15:54-55, for example; see Joseph R. Dodson, *The "Powers" of Personification in the* Book of Wisdom *and the Letter to the Romans* (BZNW 161; Berlin: de Gruyter, 2008), 119-39 for Paul's personification of Sin and Death in Rom 5-7. Whether or not Paul actually conceived of the Sin, Death, etc. as demonic powers is a debated issue, as Dodson acknowledges, but that he at least presented them as such for

why Jesus, as he dies, asks God why he has forsaken him (ὁ θεός μου ὁ θεός μου, εἰς τί ἐγκατέλιπές με; ["My God, my God, why have you forsaken me?"]; 15:34). The unspoken answer is so that Jesus may be given over to demonic forces, including death itself.[28] It also explains why Mark introduces Jesus's urgent inquiry, which the centurion hears (15:39), with ἐβόησεν ὁ Ἰησοῦς φωνῇ μεγάλῃ ("Jesus bellowed with a great cry"; cf. 15:37), a phrase that ironically echoes Legion's own urgently interrogative response upon first seeing his enemy Jesus in 5:7: κράξας φωνῇ μεγάλῃ λέγει τί ἐμοὶ καὶ σοί, Ἰησοῦ υἱὲ τοῦ θεοῦ τοῦ ὑψίστου; ("having shrieked with a great cry: 'what do you and I have in common, Jesus, son of the most high God?'").[29] Much in every way, it turns out, for just as Jesus facilitates the destruction of the monstrous Legion, so does the demonic centurion, a few chapters later, oversee Jesus's death on a cross. Before, the demons were at the mercy of Jesus, who freed their victim from the cavernous tombs in which they held him. Now, Jesus is at the mercy of the demons, at least until the giant stone is miraculously removed from the cavern in which he and (metaphorically) all mortals are entombed and he emerges from it alive (see 16:4-6).[30]

---

rhetorical effect is uncontested. For a classic, if tendentious, statement of the problem, see Rudolf Bultmann, *The Theology of the New Testament* (trans. Kendrick Grobel; 2 vols.; New York: Scribners, 1951-1955), 1:244-45.

[28] One is reminded of King Saul's experience, when God's spirit departs and an evil spirit immediately begins to torment him (1 Sam 16:14).

[29] For this understanding of the Greek, see Marcus, *Mark*, 1:187.

[30] The Cyclopeia's relevance to the story of Jesus's death, burial, and resurrection is all the more plausible when one recognizes that in Homer, Odysseus's escape from Polyphemus's cave symbolizes the hero's rebirth, as do other elements in the series of events he recounts to the Phaeacians. See George E. Dimock, Jr., "The Name of Odysseus," *Essays on the Odyssey: Select Modern Criticism* (ed. Charles H. Taylor, Jr.; Bloomington: Indiana University Press, 1963), 54-72, here 59; Schein, "Odysseus and Polyphemus," 82-83; and Pura Nieto Hernández, "Back in

The Empty Tomb as a Cyclopeian Motif

The Homeric allusions that MacDonald observes thus map onto a coherent, if somewhat schematic theological interpretation of Jesus's ministry, death, and resurrection, and are in fact integral in communicating Mark's Christology to his ancient readers. This functionality allows for a convincing explanation of the peculiarity of some of Mark's compositional decisions, in particular his choice to focus exclusively on the empty tomb as a sign of Jesus's resurrection. The strangeness of this decision is rarely granted sufficient weight. If one accepts that Mark originally and intentionally ended at 16:8 — surely a reasonable conclusion from the manuscript evidence, even if a contested one[31] — then Mark decides not merely to omit such stories from his Gospel, but to supplant them with a tradition of Jesus's empty tomb. Paul presents the risen Christ's appearances as universally acknowledged traditions (1 Cor 15:3-7), which makes it difficult to believe Mark would not have known them, even if one doubts the emerging consensus that Mark knew Paul's writings or theology.[32] Moreover, Paul finds such accounts of the risen Christ's appearances sufficiently authoritative to refer to them as all

---

the Cave of the Cyclops," *AJP* 121.3 (2000): 345-66, here 353-54. Also relevant is Rick M. Newton, "The Rebirth of Odysseus" *GRBS* 25.1 (1984): 5-20, although Newton is more concerned with the setting in which these stories are told than with the stories themselves.

[31] For a brief discussion of the history and contours of this debate, see Nicholas P. Lunn, *The Original Ending of Mark: A New Case for the Authenticity of Mark 16:9-20* (Eugene: Wipf and Stock, 2014), 1-20.

[32] Most importantly, see Joel Marcus, "Mark — Interpreter of Paul," *NTS* 46.4 (2000): 473-87. Two recent collections of essays explore the problem in depth: *Paul and Mark: Comparative Essays Part I: Two Authors at the Beginning of Christianity* (ed. Oda Wischmeyer, David C. Sim, and Ian J. Elmer; BZNW 198; Berlin: de Gruyter, 2014) and *Mark and Paul: Comparative Essays Part II: For and Against Pauline Influence on Mark* (ed. Eve-Marie Becker, Troels Engberg-Pedersen, and Mogens Müller; BZNW 199; Berlin: de Gruyter, 2014).

but conclusive evidence that Jesus rose from the dead when he wants to persuade his readers of this in 1 Corinthians. He makes only the barest possible gesture (if that) toward empty tomb traditions in the lone word ἐτάφη ("buried") mentioned in 1 Cor 15:4.[33] Indeed, other than this, no pre-Markan evidence of the empty tomb tradition is extant. Thus, Mark's elimination of the well-known material, combined with his supplementation of it with possibly innovative and, as I will show, certainly far less compelling evidence of Jesus's resurrection,[34] constitutes a problem not merely of Markan interpretation, but also for the theory of Markan priority. Traditionally formulated, this theory places much weight on the idea that Mark's lack of significant material from Matthew and Luke is most easily explained as evidence of his ignorance of these Gospels, so that similarities between the three suggest that Matthew and Luke used his Gospel as a source, rather than the other way around.[35] In Mark's account of Jesus's

---

[33] For positive consideration of this possibility, see Ronald J. Sider, "St. Paul's Understanding of the Nature and Significance of the Resurrection in 1 Corinthians XV 1-19," *NovT* 19.2 (1977): 124-41, here 134-36, and N. T. Wright, *The Resurrection of the Son of God* (Christian Origins and the Question of God 3; Minneapolis: Fortress, 2003), 321-22. This approach seems to me to make ἐτάφη carry too much weight, but I do find compelling the idea that Paul's reference to Jesus's burial in the context of his proclamation of the resurrection implies that he and other early believers presumed the risen Christ left behind his place of burial, even if it indicates no specific knowledge of or interest in the empty tomb as revelatory of Christ's resurrection.

[34] Bart D. Ehrman's *How Jesus Became God: The Exaltation of a Jewish Preacher from Galilee* (San Francisco: HarperCollins, 2014) presents an eminently reasonable discussion of the (im)plausibility of Mark's account of Jesus's burial (151-69). For the possibility that Mark invents the empty tomb, see, e.g., John Dominic Crossan, "Empty Tomb and Absent Lord (Mark 16:1-8)," *The Passion in Mark: Studies on Mark 14-16* (ed. Werner H. Kelber; Philadelphia: Fortress, 1976), 135-52.

[35] See, e.g., B. F. Streeter's assessment of the theory of Matthean priority: "only a lunatic would leave out Matthew's account of the Infancy,

resurrection, the Second Evangelist chooses to omit something he must have known about and whose significance to the Gospel's proclamation could hardly be more significant: Jesus's post-mortem appearances to his followers. If he is capable of omitting these, why not also the Sermon on the Mount or the parable of the Good Samaritan, or virtually anything else one finds in Matthew or Luke, but not in Mark? Why, in short, bother to posit Markan priority? Much hangs on a persuasive accounting for Mark's peculiar conclusion.

In offering one, it is first of all important to recognize that the vacancy of Jesus's tomb fails to establish that Jesus rose from the dead, a fact even Mark's earliest extant interpreter recognized.[36] Matthew appends to Mark's account

---

the sermon on the Mount, and practically all of the parables, in order to get room for" the kind of "verbal expansion" characteristic of Mark's literary style (*The Four Gospels: A Study of Origins, Treating of the Manuscript Tradition, Sources, Authorship, & Dates* [rev. ed.; London: Macmillan, 1936], 158). For a somewhat more nuanced assessment, which nonetheless comes to basically the same conclusion, see Robert H. Stein, *Studying the Synoptic Gospels: Origin and Interpretation* (2nd ed.; Grand Rapids: Baker Academic, 2001), 55–56.

[36] Collins's argument to the contrary fails to persuade. "Since the absence of Jesus's body could be explained in a variety of ways, Mark chose to express the significance of that absence by portraying a 'young man' taking the role of an interpreting angel. This standard apocalyptic character makes clear that the women have come to the right tomb and that Jesus's body has not been removed or stolen. Rather, the crucified one is risen" (*Mark*, 781–82). The "young man" sitting on the right side of the entrance to Jesus's tomb in 16:5-7 is more plausibly identified as the "young man" who fled at the moment of Jesus's violent arrest a little earlier (14:51-52) than he is an angel. Both figures are designated as νεανίσκος, and both are described with reference to their clothing. Moreover, the young man in Mark 16 does not give authoritative testimony of Jesus's resurrection: he makes no claims to autopsy, let alone to divinely revealed knowledge. On the contrary, he merely points to the crucified Christ's self-evidently empty tomb (16:6) and quotes what Jesus himself had prophesied shortly before his arrest, going so far as to cite

of the empty tomb an episode that anticipates and responds to the reasonable objection that Jesus's body was not resurrected from his tomb, but rather removed by a disciple (Matt 28:11-15). He proceeds to integrate the empty tomb narrative into a lengthier account of Jesus's resurrection (Matt 28), which includes reports of the risen Jesus's appearances to his followers such as those Paul mentions as common knowledge in the opening verses of 1 Cor 15. The other evangelists do the same (Luke 24; John 20-21), as they must in order to give their accounts of Jesus's empty tomb any power to persuade readers that Jesus rose. In light of Mark's neglect of all this, it seems reasonable to conclude that Mark never meant for his

---

Jesus as his source: ἀλλ' ὑπάγετε εἴπατε τοῖς μαθηταῖς αὐτοῦ καὶ τῷ Πέτρῳ ὅτι προάγει ὑμᾶς εἰς τὴν Γαλιλαίαν· ἐκεῖ αὐτὸν ὄψεσθε, καθὼς εἶπεν ὑμῖν (16:7; cf. 14:28: ἀλλὰ μετὰ τὸ ἐγερθῆναί με προάξω ὑμᾶς εἰς τὴν Γαλιλαίαν). Even the addition of Peter's name here may be explained with reference to Jesus's words in Mark 14, for immediately after announcing his impending resurrection and appearances in Galilee, Jesus goes on to prophesy that Peter will deny that he was one of his followers (14:29-31).

The young man mentioned at the scene of Jesus's arrest in 14:50-52 had apparently been present when Jesus spoke to his disciples on the Mount of Olives just hours before (14:27-31). This young man—the first of Jesus's followers to flee—is also the first to trust in Jesus's prophetic insistence that he would be vindicated from death, apparently upon seeing Jesus's empty tomb. He urges the women to repeat Jesus's prophetic words to the disciples (with Peter excluded from their number because the discourse they are to repeat had included a prophecy that Peter would himself deny being a disciple), and he encourages them to trust that what Jesus said is true and that it explains the empty tomb they have encountered.

In sum, the young man is a figure of faith in the truth of Jesus's promises of resurrection; he does not present authoritative testimony to their truth. He and the empty tomb combine to present a final call to faith, rather than an explanation of emptiness as decisive evidence of Jesus's resurrection.

account of the empty tomb to have such persuasive power. It must serve a different purpose.[37]

The Cronos-Zeus Myth and Mark

Rather than establishing the veracity of Jesus's resurrection, Jesus's empty tomb in Mark gestures at the theological implications of his escape from death by introducing a mythical paradigm suggesting how the skeletal redemptive Christology Mark's Gospel presents might be fleshed out. As I shall show, some of Mark's early readers seem to have followed his suggestions, whether consciously or not. Central to this paradigm is the Cyclopeia, to be sure, but the Cyclopeia itself seems to invoke and revise another myth, first extant in Hesiod (*Theog.* 453–506) but reported elsewhere as well. According to this story, the god Zeus is saved by his mother Rhea and by Gaia from his father, the Titan Cronos, who devours all of Zeus's Olympian siblings in an attempt to secure his cosmic reign from potential rivals. Rhea and Gaia hide the infant Zeus away in a cave until he grows to maturity and then somehow trick Cronos into mistaking a great stone for the young god, which the Titan consumes but later vomits forth with the other gods in connection with Zeus's mature emergence from the cave in which he was hidden. Zeus defeats Cronos, liberates the other Olympians, and assumes monarchical authority in Cronos's stead, placing the stone Cronos had swallowed and regurgitated in Pytho as a monument to all that had happened. This well-known story's parallels with the Cyclopeia are obvious, extensive, and have

---

[37] Explanations of the empty tomb's functionality in Mark other than the one I will propose have been offered. For example, see Helmut Koester, "On Heroes, Tombs, and Early Christianity: An Epilogue," *Flavius Philostratus*: *Heroikos* (trans. Jennifer K. Berenson Maclean and Ellen Bradshaw Aitken; WGRW 1; Atlanta: Society of Biblical Literature, 2001), 257–64.

frequently been noted—there is no need to go over them here.³⁸ It seems plausible that Mark too observed them and that he crafted his Gospel's conclusion so that its numerous and diverse mythical resonances would reverberate and amplify certain theological suggestions made earlier in his narrative.

The same heroic parallels between Jesus and Odysseus hold for Jesus and Zeus, who like Odysseus saves himself and his comrades from a monstrous anthropophagic enemy. The Hesiodic story, however, adds the theme of divine salvation to this paradigm, for the old gods Rhea and Gaia hide Zeus away, and Gaia also plays a role in bringing him out of the cave to confront Cronos (see *Theog.* 493-96), although the means by which she deceives Cronos in order to ensure that he γόνον ἄψ ἀνέηκε ("threw up his offspring"; 495) is unclear.³⁹ Similarly, Mark's prophecies that Jesus or the Son of Man will rise seem to gesture vaguely at God's role in raising him from the dead (8:31; 9:9, 31; 10:34; see also 14:28, where Jesus speaks of his resurrection as τὸ ἐγερθῆναί με, which should probably be taken as a divine passive),⁴⁰ although here also the mechanism of his restoration to life is left obscure. Moreover, Zeus emerges from his cave both to defeat

---

³⁸ E.g., Justin Glenn, "The Polyphemus Myth: Its Origin and Interpretation," *GR* 25.2 (1978): 141-55 and Hernández, "Back in the Cave."

³⁹ I quote Friedrich Solmsen et al., ed., *Hesiodi Opera* (3rd ed.; OCT; Oxford: Clarendon, 1990). Other versions of the myth remove Gaia from this part, or replace her with Metis: Zeus emerges from the cave full-grown, marries Metis, and then they (presumably deceptively) give Cronus a drug that induces vomiting in order to save the other Olympians (see Apollodorus, *Library* 1.2). This version recalls Odysseus's serving of alcohol to the Cyclops, which not only induces sleep, but leads to his vomiting up bits and pieces of the hero's devoured comrades (φάρυγος δ' ἐξέσσυτο οἶνος /ψωμοί τ' ἀνδρόμεοι· ὁ δ' ἐρεύγετο οἰνοβαρείων, *Od.* 9.371-74).

⁴⁰ Gundry, *Mark*, 848.

powerful Cronos and to rule the gods in his stead. Likewise, Mark prophesies that the vindicated Son of Man who rises will rule at God's right hand, and that the heavenly powers will tremble when he assumes that position of authority (see 13:24–26; cf. 8:31–9:1).

These theologically resonant parallels to the myth of Cronos and Zeus, secondary to but latent in Mark's subtle engagements with the Cyclopeia, point to a comprehensive understanding of the Markan Jesus's redemptive death and resurrection. Under the direction of God (14:35–36), the divine man Jesus executes a dangerous plan. He deceives the demonic powers, including death, by presenting himself as a ransom for their many human thralls (10:45), all the while trusting that God will shortly deliver him from those enemies by raising him from the dead: μετὰ τρεῖς ἡμέρας ἀναστῆναι ("after three days he will rise"; 8:31; 9:31; 10:34). Although it may indicate a final moment of doubt that God really will raise him from the dead, in the mythical context I have been exploring, Jesus's troubling cry of dereliction (15:34) looks like a ploy to trick his carefully observant enemies into imagining that he has in fact submitted to their power, when he is really biding his time until his escape and their defeat. The centurion's gloating response to his words would indicate that the deception worked. Recall that in Homer, Odysseus served wine to Polyphemus in order deceptively to prevent the monster from consuming him and his companions (*Od.* 9.345–74), while in Hesiod, Gaia deceptively served the great rock to Cronos to keep him from eating Zeus (*Theog.* 485–92). In a striking revision of this mythical paradigm, Jesus deceives his demonic enemies and saves his companions by actually presenting himself as a meal to the anthropophagic powers in exchange for their liberation, with the cannibalistic understanding of Jesus's death made explicit in Jesus's proleptic commemoration of his impending death for his followers at the Last Supper:⁴¹

> λαβὼν ἄρτον εὐλογήσας ἔκλασεν ... καὶ εἶπεν ... τοῦτό ἐστιν τὸ σῶμά μου. καὶ λαβὼν ποτήριον εὐχαριστήσας ... καὶ ἔπιον ἐξ αὐτοῦ πάντες. καὶ εἶπεν αὐτοῖς· τοῦτό ἐστιν τὸ αἷμά μου ... τὸ ἐκχυννόμενον ὑπὲρ πολλῶν.
>
> Taking the bread he blessed and broke it ... and he said ... this is my body. And taking the cup he gave thanks ... and they all drank from it. And he said to them, this is my blood ... poured out for many.⁴² (14:22–24)

Jesus, though, trusts that God will deliver him from the demons and from hypostasized death, as his numerous predictions of resurrection indicate.⁴³ Mark's closing notice of the great stone rolled away from the cave in which he had

---

⁴¹ See also 6:14–29, which analogously presents John the Baptist's passion in a cannibalistic context.

⁴² Mark's particular transformation of the Cyclopeia resolves the same problem Vergil identified and addressed in his revision of it. Odysseus fails to save several of his men; in fact, one might argue that he uses their deaths to save himself, for his plan involves serving Polyphemus wine with the final meal the monster makes of his companions (*Od.* 9.347-49). Vergil underscores and expands Odysseus's callousness toward his fellows by actually having him leave one behind on the island, and he complementarily arranges for his hero Aeneas to save the man Odysseus had left behind, thereby showing himself superior to his self-interested predecessor. Jesus more radically undoes Odysseus's selfishness, by himself becoming the meal that allows his followers to avoid consumption by the anthropophagic monster.

⁴³ Perhaps this explains Jesus's very different responses to interrogation by the high priest, to whom he boldly predicts the Son of Man's vindication (14:53–65), and by Pontius Pilate, to whom Jesus seems reticent to say anything at all (15:1–5). Since Mark, as argued above, conventionally associates Jesus's demonic enemies with Roman authorities, in speaking before them, Jesus must be careful to avoid giving away the redemptive plan. When he speaks to Jewish authorities, however, such care is not necessary, for they are not demonic.

been buried, with that cavernous tomb now miraculously empty, suggests that Jesus was not disappointed.

Anthropophagic Redemption as Ancient Markan Reception

While the deception of the anthropophagic enemy remains implicit in Mark's adaptation of the earlier mythical material, it is intriguing and perhaps significant that this theme emerges clearly in early Christian interpretations of and elaborations on the theology of Jesus's redemptive death and resurrection that Mark sketches out in his discrete Christological statements (3:27; 10:45) and his more developed narrative treatment. Gregory of Nyssa, for instance, writes of Jesus's death and resurrection that

> ὡς ἂν εὔληπτον γένοιτο τῷ ἐπιζητοῦντι ὑπὲρ ἡμῶν τὸ ἀντάλλαγμα, τῷ προκαλύμματι τῆς φύσεως ἡμῶν ἐνεκρύφθη τὸ θεῖον, ἵνα κατὰ τοὺς λίχνους τῶν ἰχθύων τῷ δελέατι τῆς σαρκὸς συγκατασπασθῇ τὸ ἄγκιστρον τῆς θεότητος, καὶ οὕτω τῆς ζωῆς τῷ θανάτῳ εἰσοικισθείσης καὶ τῷ σκότῳ τοῦ φωτὸς ἐπιφανέντος ἐξαφανισθῇ τὸ τῷ φωτὶ καὶ τῇ ζωῇ κατὰ τὸ ἐναντίον νοούμενον· οὐ γὰρ ἔχει φύσιν οὔτε σκότος διαμένειν ἐν φωτὸς παρουσίᾳ οὔτε θάνατον εἶναι ζωῆς ἐνεργούσης.[44]

> Therefore, in order to secure that the ransom on our behalf might be easily accepted by him who required it, the Deity was hidden under the veil of our nature, that so, as with ravenous fish, the hook of the Deity might be gulped down along with the bait of flesh, and thus, life being introduced into the house of death, and light shining in darkness, that which is diametrically opposed to light and life might vanish; for it is not in the nature of darkness to remain when light is present,

---

[44] I quote Ekkehard Mühlenberg, ed., *Gregorii Nysseni Oratio Catechetica: Opera Dogmatica Minora, Pars IV* (Collegium Patristicum ab Academiis Gottingensi Heidelbergensi Moguntina Monacensi Institutum; Leiden: Brill, 1996).

or of death to exist when life is active.⁴⁵ (*Oratio Catechetica* 65 M [24])

To cite just three additional examples, one finds the same line of interpretation in John of Damascus (*De fide orthodoxa* 3.27), who follows Gregory closely, although he has Death take the bait; in Gregory the Great (*Moral.* 33.7), where Satan, in the guise of Job 40's Behemoth, takes the bait; and in Cyril of Jerusalem (*Catechetical Lectures* 12.15), where Jesus's body becomes a deadly bait in order that death itself, figured as a dragon, might in its hope to devour it be tricked into disgorging those who have already been consumed: δέλεαρ τοίνυν τοῦ θανάτου γέγονε τὸ σῶμα, ἵνα ἐλπίσας καταπιεῖν ὁ δράκων ἐξεμέσῃ καὶ τοὺς ἤδη καταποθέντας.⁴⁶ In all these and other patristic writings, Satan or a hypostasized death is figured as an anthropophagic beast or monster that devours divinity hidden within humanity, and in so doing finds itself destroyed by the Lord of Life it was tricked into consuming, forced into disgorging not only Christ, but others as well.⁴⁷ The theme of divine victory over an anthropophagic enemy by means of a deceptive feeding that turns a demonic enemy's destructive appetites against it becomes increasingly explicit as later Christian theologians imaginatively develop the redemptive Christology that Mark helped originate. While it would be wrong to propose a single original impulse for this

---

⁴⁵ Gregory of Nyssa, *Select Writings and Letters of Gregory, Bishop of Nyssa* (trans. William Moore and Henry Austin Wilson; NPNF² 5; 1893; repr., Peabody, MA: Hendrickson, 1994), 494 (slightly altered).

⁴⁶ I quote Joseph Rupp, ed., *S. Cyrilli opera quae supersunt omnia*, vol. 2. Munich: Sumptibus Librariae Lentnerianae, 1860; (repr., Hildesheim: Olms, 1967).

⁴⁷ For an discussion of this literary-theological theme in early Christian writing, see Linda Munk, *Devil's Mousetrap: Redemption and Colonial American Literature* (Oxford: Oxford University Press, 1997), 3–23, especially 19–23. See also Aulén, *Christus Victor*, 47–55.

early and widespread—though to much modern Christian thinking, highly peculiar—theological conceptualization of the atonement,[48] it seems plausible that Mark's redemptive literary engagements with the Cyclopeia and related "pagan" mythical traditions in his narrative of Jesus's ministry, death, and resurrection encouraged early readers of his and the other Gospels to develop explanations of Jesus's redemptive death and resurrection in terms of mythical scenarios analogous to those Mark adapted. I see every reason to suspect that, in so doing, they were responding to subtle Markan cues about how best to interpret the story he originally wrote.

Homeric Epic in Mark's Gospel and Philostratus's *Life of Apollonius*

A text closely related to Mark displays a pattern of Homeric echoes analogous to what MacDonald and I find in Mark and its interpretive tradition. Formal and structural similarities between Philostratus's *Life of Apollonius* and the New Testament Gospels have sometimes suggested to readers that the former relies on the latter, although most biblical scholars familiar with the *Life* probably would not accept that conclusion, instead imagining the connections to be generic, or explicable with reference to literary commonplaces that both

---

[48] See, for instance, Laurence W. Grensted, *A Short History of the Doctrine of the Atonement* (Manchester: Manchester University Press, 1920), 32-55, which clearly regards the idea as an antiquarian curiosity, insufficient to do any genuine theological work. I do not share this dismissive attitude toward the theological conception, and I suspect that responses like Grensted's primarily register the fact that the theory resonates within a Greco-Roman mythical context normally prejudged to be theologically absurd, if not perverse. In any case, Mark seems to have been more interested in redeeming than in dismissing or condemning this mythical tradition.

the Gospels and the *Life* supposedly incorporate.⁴⁹ Certainly, some such explanation of the parallels is necessary, for Philostratus's early third-century story of the holy man Apollonius resembles Mark and the other Gospels quite closely in specific details and passages, including in their accounts of exorcisms, such as the Markan episode with which this essay began (compare, e.g., *Life* 4.20 and Mark 8:22–26; 10:46–62).

My analysis of the *Life* will ultimately focus on Philostratean analogues to the evangelical passion narrative, but I begin by noting a general similarity that has received no attention at all: Mark and Philostratus employ Homeric epic similarly, invoking it in an extensive series of allusions that invite readers to compare and contrast their works' heroes (Jesus and Apollonius) to the Odyssean paradigm. In a fascinating essay on the *Life of Apollonius*, Gert-Jan van Dijk studies this allusive pattern quite carefully and comes to interpretive conclusions that closely resemble and complement MacDonald's work on Mark.⁵⁰ Of course, the works of Mark and Philostratus are stylistically quite different: Philostratus, associated with the Second Sophistic

---

⁴⁹ See, e.g., Erkki Koskenniemi, *Apollonios von Tyana in der neutestamentlichen Exegese: Forschungsbericht und Weiterführung der Diskussion* (WUNT II/61; Tübingen: Mohr Siebeck, 1994), 189–206. Arguments for Apollonius's dependence on the Gospels include Ferdinand Christian Baur, "Apollonius von Tyana und Christus oder das Verhältniss des Pythagoreismus zum Christentum. Ein Beitrag zur Religionsgeschichte der ersten Jarhunderte nach Christus," *Drei Abhandlungen zur Geschichte der alten Philosophie und ihres Verhältnisses zum Christentum* (ed. Eduard Zeller; Leipzig: Fues's Verlag, 1876), 1–227 (passim) and Gertrud Herzog-Hauser, "Die Tendenzen der Apollonius-Biographie," *Jahrbuch der österreichischen Leo-Gesellschaft* (1930): 177–200.

⁵⁰ Gert-Jan van Dijk, "The *Odyssey* of Apollonius: An Intertextual Paradigm," *Philostratus* (ed. Ewen Bowie and Jaś Elsner; Greek Culture in the Roman World; Cambridge: Cambridge University Press, 2009), 176–202.

movement, writes in elegant Atticizing Greek and his hero is himself deeply familiar with Homeric writings, which leads to clearer citation of Homer and less obscure echoes than those found in Mark. But such stylistic differences aside, the overarching approach to Homer that Van Dijk and MacDonald independently argue each text adopts is basically identical.

It thus will come as little surprise that, as in Mark, so in Philostratus one finds two interrelated allusions to the story of Odysseus's confrontation with Polyphemus (*Life* 4.36; 7.28).[51] Both Philostratean allusions figure Apollonius as Odysseus and a Roman emperor—Nero in the first and Domitian in the latter—as the Cyclops. The former underscores Apollonius's heroic bravery in proceeding to Rome, even though he is aware that monstrous Nero awaits him. The philosopher Philolaus first introduces the comparison between Nero and Polyphemus when he meets Apollonius, who is heading to Rome while he is going in the opposite direction. Having fled the emperor, he warns Apollonius that Νέρων σε ὠμὸν φάγοι ("Nero will eat you raw"), specifying that ἔσται σοι τὸ ἐντυχεῖν αὐτῷ καὶ ἐπὶ πλείονι ἢ τῷ Ὀδυσσεῖ ἐγένετο, ὁπότε παρὰ τὸν Κύκλωπα ἦλθεν ("It will be for you when you happen upon him worse than it was for Odysseus when he came to the Cyclops"; 4.36.3).[52] Apollonius's rejoinder elaborates Philolaus's Homeric allusion to express confidence that he will triumph: οἴει . . . τοῦτον ἧττον ἐκτετυφλῶσεσθαι

---

[51] Van Dijk, "The *Odyssey* of Apollonius," 179–81.

[52] I reluctantly quote Philostratus, *Apollonius of Tyana* (ed. Christopher P. Jones; 3 vols.; LCL; Cambridge, MA: Harvard University Press, 2005). Jones's edition is limited, but there is no proper critical edition of this important text. Hopefully, Gerard Boter will rectify this problem. See his "Towards a New Critical Edition of Philostratus' *Life of Apollonius*: The Affiliation of the Manuscripts," *Theios Sophistes: Essays on Flavius Philostratus' Vita Apollonii* (ed. Kristoffel Demoen and Danny Praet; Leiden: Brill, 2009), 21–56.

τοῦ Κύκλωπος, εἰ τοιαῦτα ἐργάζεται; ("Do you think that this man will be blinded any less than the Cyclops was, if he does such things?") When Apollonius is subsequently brought up on charges of impiety against Nero in Rome (4.44.1), he responds to interrogation at the hands of Nero's lackey Tigellinus with a riposte that recalls his earlier reference to Odysseus's blinding of Polyphemus, while at the same time comparing Nero to a demon. The written accusation against Apollonius, which Tigellinus shakes at him as if brandishing a weapon, miraculously dissolves, so that upon opening the scroll Tigellinus ἀσήμῳ δέ τινι βιβλίῳ ἐνέτυχεν ("met a document lacking any writing"; 4.44.2). Prevented from seeing the accusation (i.e., blinded, like Polyphemus), he begins to interrogate Apollonius regarding his supposed congress with demons: Τοὺς <δὲ> δαίμονας . . . πῶς ἐλέγχεις; ("how do you... bring demons to the test?"; 4.44.3). Apollonius responds, ὥς γε... τοὺς μιαιφόνους τε καὶ ἀσεβεῖς ἀνθρώπους ("in the same way... I do murderous and impious men"), which Philostratus glosses with this comment: ταυτὶ δὲ πρὸς τὸν Τιγελλῖνον ἀποσκοπῶν ἔλεγεν, ἐπειδὴ πάσης ὠμότητός τε καὶ ἀσελγείας διδάσκαλος ἦν τῷ Νέρωνι ("These things he spoke with regard for Tigellinus, since he was Nero's teacher of all savagery and wanton violence"; 4.44.3). Immediately thereafter, Tigellinus lets Apollonius go, convinced by the holy man's claim that he could not be imprisoned (4.44.4).

In both Mark 5 and *Life of Apollonius* 4.36, 44, the authors frame their heroes' entrances into enemy territory and subsequent conflicts with adversaries as versions of Odysseus sailing to the island of the Cyclopes and doing battle there with Polyphemus. In Mark, the Polyphemus-like enemy is transformed into a demoniac, although a more-subtle connection with Roman imperial power is implied. In Apollonius, analogously, the defeated Cyclopean enemy becomes the Roman emperor Nero — in the person of Nero's henchman Tigellinus—and is also suggestively assimilated to a demoniac.

The second allusion to the Cyclopeia in Philostratus's *Life* occurs in a similar context. Soon before Apollonius is summoned from prison to Domitian's presence for questioning, a man visits him to offer advice regarding how Domitian will appear and to encourage him not to fear (7.28.2). The holy man replies:

> Ὀδυσσεὺς μέντοι . . . παριὼν ἐς τὸ τοῦ Πολυφήμου ἄντρον, καὶ μηδ' ὁπόσος ἐστὶ προακηκοὼς πρότερον, μηδ' οἷα σιτεῖται, μηδ' ὡς βροντᾷ ἡ φωνή, ἐθάρρησέ τε αὐτὸν καίτοι ἐν ἀρχῇ δείσας καὶ ἀθῆλθε τοῦ ἄντρου ἀνὴρ δόξας, ἐμοὶ δὲ ἐξελθεῖν αὔταρκες ἐμαυτόν τε σώσαντα καὶ τοὺς ἑταίρους, ὑπὲρ ὧν κινδυνεύω.

> To be sure, Odysseus . . . when going into Polyphemus's cave, heard no report beforehand as to how great he was, nor about what sorts of things he ate, nor about how his voice thundered, and he felt confident against him (although at the beginning he was afraid) and he left the cave showing himself to be a man. It is sufficient for me to leave having saved myself and my companions, on whose account I am in danger. (7.28.3)

Apollonius's planned departure is realized when, after handling himself skillfully in his hearing before Domitian, he escapes the emperor's court δαιμόνιόν τε καὶ οὐ ῥᾴδιον εἰπεῖν τρόπον ("in a way both miraculous and not easy to explain"; 8.8). He suddenly appears in the presence of his disciples, who are mourning their master, for they assume he has been unjustly condemned to death (8.11–12). These disciples do not initially recognize Apollonius and when they do, they believe him to be a ghost until he invites them to touch his body (8.12). The parallels with the New Testament accounts of the risen Jesus's appearances to his disciples are extensive and obvious. Though they more specifically suggest connections with Luke (24:13-35) and John (20:24-29) than with Mark, since Jesus's death and resurrection in all the canonical Gospels follows on the heels of an unjust trial before a Roman imperial representative, the points of contact between Apollonius's miraculous salvation from the unjust imperial hearing expected to culminate in his execution, on the one hand, and the basic evangelical pattern of Jesus's miraculous resurrection after his trial and execution, on the other, are still sufficiently striking.

What Philostratus shares in common with Mark in particular is also significant: a second allusion to the Cyclopeia that serves to underscore the heroic magnitude of the holy man's miraculous escape from death at his adversary's hands. In the *Life*, Domitian, the Roman enemy threatening the hero with death, is explicitly assimilated to Polyphemus. Similarly, in Mark, the death to which Jesus is given over by the demonic Roman authorities (the centurion who oversees Jesus's execution and Pontius Pilate, who orders it and subsequently permits the body's entombment; 15:43-45) is likened to Polyphemus's cave, from which Jesus, like Odysseus, manages to escape.

One might conclude from all this merely that the Polyphemus *topos* independently came to the mind of writers seeking to emphasize their heroes' triumph over evil enemies.[53] But the specificity of the connections I have noted between the Cyclopeia and both Mark and Apollonius — e.g., not just between Polyphemus and evil, but Polyphemus and evil specifically marked as Roman — perhaps require a more robust explanation and deserve more careful consideration. Koskenniemi's authoritative statement to the contrary notwithstanding,[54] the question of the Gospels' relationship to

---

[53] For a brief discussion of other ancient engagements with this Homeric episode, see MacDonald, *Homeric Epics*, 67.

[54] See Koskenniemi, *Apollonios von Tyana*, 203.

Apollonius should remain open and might be more productively explored within the broader context of post-classical Greek literature's engagement with scriptural authority, than with the methodically constricted source-critical approaches to the Gospels that New Testament scholars have traditionally employed.[55] It is to reflection on this broader context that I now turn.

Homer as Critically Received Scripture

In a study of Stoic allegorical interpretation of Homer, A. A. Long notes that Homer's status in Greco-Roman Mediterranean culture was analogous to the Bible's in ancient Jewish and Christian communities.[56] More recently, Margalit Finkelberg has developed this comparison systematically,[57] by

---

[55] On these methodologies' inability to discern, let alone to comprehend or interpret, the kinds of imitative literary relationships I explore in this essay (which were widely recognized in the ancient world), see Adam Winn, *Mark and the Elijah-Elisha Narrative: Considering the Practice of Greco-Roman Imitation in the Search for Markan Source Material* (Eugene: Wipf and Stock, 2010), 1–10.

[56] This paragraph and its notes more-or-less reproduce a paragraph from Austin Busch "Gnostic Biblical and Second Sophistic Homeric Interpretation," ZAC 22.2 (2018): 195-217, here 196-197. That article and its companion, "Characterizing Gnostic Scriptural Interpretation," ZAC 21.2 (2017): 243-271 develop more systematically the ideas I briefly present here. See A. A. Long, "Stoic Readings of Homer," *Homer's Ancient Readers: The Hermeneutics of Greek Epic's Earliest Exegetes* (ed. Robert Lamberton and John J. Keany; Princeton: Princeton University Press, 1992), 41–66, here 41–45. Long articulates a position classicists equally familiar with traditional western attitudes toward the Bible and ancient Mediterranean attitudes toward Homeric epic long have held. See, for example, Edward Gibbon, "On the *Fasti* of Ovid," *The Miscellaneous Works of Edward Gibbons, Esquire: With Memoirs of His Life and Writings* (ed. John Lord Sheffield; vol. 4; London: John Murray, 1814), 354–58, here 358.

[57] Margalit Finkelberg, "Homer as a Foundation Text," *Homer, the Bible, and Beyond: Literary and Religious Canons in the Ancient World* (ed. Margalit Finkelberg and Guy G. Stromasa; JSRC 2; Leiden: Brill, 2003), 75–

establishing criteria to determine a text's "foundational" or canonical status and then showing that Homeric epic and the Bible uniquely meet those criteria in Mediterranean antiquity. I will not summarize her arguments, but merely affirm with her that whether we consider the centrality of Homeric epic and the Hebrew Bible/Septuagint to Greco-Roman and Jewish-Christian education, respectively; the tendency to invoke these corpora as authoritative and foundational in discussions of cultural and religious identity; or the range and types of editorial and interpretive activity applied to them, including a general tendency to read the two corpora charitably, even when doing so strains the interpretive imagination[58] — from whatever point of view we examine

---

96 and Margalit Finkelberg, "Canonising and Decanonising Homer," *Homer and the Bible in the Eyes of Ancient Interpreters* (ed. Maren R. Niehoff; JSRC 16; Leiden: Brill, 2012), 15–28. In a similar vein, see also the beginning of Froma I. Zeitlin's extensive essay on Homer in imperial Greek culture, "Visions and Revisions of Homer," *Being Greek under Rome: Cultural Identity, the Second Sophistic and the Development of Empire* (ed. Simon Goldhill; Cambridge: Cambridge University Press, 2001), 195–266, here 195–203. Zeitlin argues that "Greek culture never developed the notion of a sacred book, whose authority would rely on its status as divine revelation and on its textual claims to unvarying truth," but at the same time she observes that Homeric epic acquires many of the primary functions and secondary cultural accretions of literary works that achieve the status of canonical scripture ("Visions and Revisions of Homer," 202).

[58] Elicitation of charitable interpretation — the tendency to privilege readings that "would yield an optimally successful text" — is often seen as an especially important marker of a text's canonical status. Long understands it to explain the impulse toward allegorical interpretation of Homer he studies in the essay cited above ("Stoic Readings of Homer"). For discussion, see Willard Van Orman Quine, *Word and Object* (Cambridge: MIT Press, 1960), 58–59 and Moshe Halbertal, *People of the Book: Canon, Meaning, and Authority* (Cambridge, MA: Harvard University Press, 1997), 27–44 (27 quoted just above). One implication of my discussion is that the elicitation of charitable interpretation is not as central to a text's canonical status as is often presumed. Even those committed to

Homeric epic and the Bible in tandem, these two bodies of literature seem to have been granted a similarly high level of authority in the ancient Mediterranean world.

Although Homer constitutes authoritative scripture for Philostratus, his interpretive approach to the *Iliad* and *Odyssey* is not always as complaisant as the examples treated above imply. In these, he invokes the *Odyssey*'s narrative authority primarily to underscore the monstrosity of his villains (the bad Roman emperors) with allusive reference to Homer's greatest monster and to emphasize the awesome power of his hero Apollonius by likening him to Odysseus in his defeat of that monster. Elsewhere in the *Life*, however, Philostratus's attitude to Homer is openly subversive, including explicit criticism of the poet for obfuscations and lies (*Life* 4.16). Apollonius asserts that Homer knew about but did not include in his epics any information regarding Palamedes because Odysseus unjustly plotted against this hero and arranged for his death: Homer, dedicated to Odysseus, wanted to cover up his favorite's crimes (4.16.6). Philostratus goes on to report that the spirit of Achilles charged Apollonius with honoring the hero Palamedes's grave in order to compensate for Homer's neglect (4.16.6). Philostratus pursues this particular Homeric critique further in another work, where he revises the *Iliad* in order to present Palamedes as a heroic paradigm superior to the models Homer provides (*Heroicus* 33). Philostratus, then, both emulates Homer and notes the poet's shortcomings, by exposing and correcting Homeric mendacity and error.

There is no such explicit critique of Homer in Mark, though MacDonald would probably argue that such critique is latent in Mark's transvaluative approach to Homeric poetry.[59]

---

upholding the authority of a particular text may interpret it polemically, as opposed to generously.

[59] For discussion, see MacDonald, *Homeric Epics*, 2, 9.

And perhaps it is significant that Mark 5 seems to reverse its Homeric model by attributing active deceit to the evil monster, rather than to the hero, and by having that deceit fail rather than succeed.[60] However, that possibility is obviated or at least diminished by the fact that Jesus passively deceives the demons by granting their request to enter the herd of pigs, which they think will preserve them although Jesus presumably knows it will lead to their destruction. As I argued above, the theme of heroic deception continues later in Mark, though it remains subtle.

One does find in Mark explicit scriptural critique closely analogous to the negative assessment of Homer that Philostratus proposes in the examples discussed just above. The Markan scriptural corpus that comes under fire is not Homeric epic, though, but rather the Septuagint. In Mark 10:1–12, Jesus observes that Moses's allowance of a man to divorce his wife by written decree and without show of cause (see Deut 24:1–4) stands in tension with God's true will regarding marriage, as revealed in Gen 1:27 and 2:24. He concludes that Moses introduced that permission because of the Israelites' hardness of heart, lest they be guilty of breaking an absolute prohibition of divorce they would perversely refuse to obey. Thus does the Mosaic legislation, far from reflecting God's will, show Moses pandering to Israel, at least in this passage of Scripture. For his part, Jesus will privilege God's plan and set himself against Mosaic law (ὃ οὖν ὁ θεὸς συνέζευξεν ἄνθρωπος μὴ χωριζέτω ["What then God has joined together let not a person rend apart"]).[61] The analogy

---

[60] See MacDonald's concluding comparison of Jesus's salvation of the monster to Odysseus's deceit and destruction of the monster in *Homeric Epics*, 74.

[61] For thorough discussion of this example of Markan scriptural interpretation, see Austin Busch, "Characterizing Gnostic Scriptural Interpretation," 260–66. Note that the analysis I offer of the dominical

between Mark's approach to the Septuagint and Philostratus's to Homer in the *Life of Apollonius* 4.16 is exceptionally precise in that both accuse scriptural authors of altering the truth to please their constituencies: in Philostratus, Homer writes to favor Odysseus; in Mark, Moses writes to please the Israelites.

Emendatory Emulation of Sacred Literature as Late Antique Hermeneutic

The scripturally emendatory impulses that Mark and the *Life of Apollonius* display evolve and expand when these writings are viewed as representative of slightly more expansive literary corpora: Second Sophistic works of Homeric revision and early Christian Biblical revisions. On the Homeric side, texts like Philostratus's *Heroicus* and Dio Chrysostom's *Trojan Oration*, and on the Biblical side, those associated with classic Gnosticism (e.g., *Hypostasis of the Archons*), present emendatory scriptural revision closely related to but far more sustained than what the *Life of Apollonius* and the Gospel of Mark attempt. For example, *The Apocryphon of John*, formally a dialogue, attributes an elaborate revision of the opening chapters of Genesis to a vision of Christ risen from the dead. The Savior constantly condemns Moses by name, draws attention to contradictions and lies the prophet introduces into the Biblical account, and offers his own elaborate emendatory elaborations. Many of these transform into villains or dupes figures Genesis basically presents positively (e.g., God), and vice versa (e.g., Eve). Similarly, Philostratus's *Heroicus*, also a dialogue, attributes a radical revision of the *Iliad* to a vision of Protesilaus risen from the dead. This hero constantly condemns Homer by name, draws attention to contradictions and lies the poet introduces into his epics, and offers his own elaborate emendations.

---

teaching's relationship to the Septuagint is not new; Ptolemy comes to the same conclusion in the *Letter to Flora* (33.4.4–10).

Many of these transform Homeric heroes into villains (e.g., Odysseus, §49) and vice versa (e.g., Achilles, 48.5-10).[62] Elsewhere I closely examine the relationship between such examples of Second Sophistic Homeric and classic Gnostic scriptural interpretation and conclude that these two intellectual movements draw on a single, coherent tradition of sustained, emendatory scriptural revision.[63]

MacDonald's innovative scholarship on Markan revision of Homer turns out to identify the tip of a hermeneutical iceberg. There existed a conventional set of approaches and practices ancient writers brought to bear on scripture, by which I mean neither the Bible nor literature in general, but rather literary corpora widely accepted as authoritative in determining religious, philosophical, and cultural norms and beliefs—Homer and the Septuagint being prime but not exclusive examples. Some of these interpretive approaches have been thoroughly studied, such as allegory; others, less so, and they accordingly seem highly idiosyncratic, even bizarre, especially when isolated from the broader scripturally interpretive matrix in which they naturally fit.[64] Accordingly, scholars of ancient Christianity and classicists alike have regularly been guilty of substituting

---

[62] Philostratus revises Homer's most troubling claims about Achilles (48.5-10). He transforms Achilles's refusal to fight on behalf of the Achaeans because of a minor dispute with Agamemnon over a slave-girl into his protest of the hero Palamedes's unjust execution, orchestrated by Odysseus and agreed to by Agamemnon. Also, he eliminates the impious and hypocritically exaggerated way in which Achilles mourns the friend whom he had allowed to fight in his stead (especially by sacrificing at his grave twelve captured Trojan youths; *Il.* 18.336-37; 23.175-76).

[63] Austin Busch, "Gnostic Biblical and Second Sophistic Homeric Interpretation."

[64] For an attempt to delimit and characterize one such approach ("sustained contrarian revision"), see Busch, "Characterizing Gnostic Scriptural Interpretation."

for careful analysis value laden judgments about the strangeness or extravagance of Gnostic revisionary Biblical and second-sophistic revisionary Homeric interpretation.[65] In fact, though, careful analysis reveals something else: these interpretive works' striking similarities constitute evidence of an ancient hermeneutical approach hardly less conventional than allegory: sustained emendatory revision as a means to critique and revise supremely authoritative scriptural writings without jettisoning their authority altogether.

MacDonald's construal of Mark as a series of hermeneutically significant reworkings of Homeric epic seems hardly less idiosyncratic to Biblical scholars than does Gnostic Biblical interpretation, and there are of course various institutional and ideological reasons for this. But, when one compares what MacDonald discovers in Mark to what classicists have noticed about Philostratus's analogous approach to Homer in the *Life of Apollonius*, or about Vergil's in the *Aeneid*, one begins to suspect that MacDonald has hit upon another convention of ancient Mediterranean scriptural interpretation, this one involving the deployment of subtle literary parallels to suggest hermeneutically significant similarities and divergences between an exceptionally pious figure (Jesus, Apollonius, or Aeneas) and scripturally authoritative heroes such as Odysseus. Adam Winn seems to complement MacDonald when he demonstrates that Mark adopts much the same hermeneutical stance toward the

---

[65] These tendencies are so commonplace that they hardly require reference. But see, for instance, Graham Anderson's dismissive statement about Dio Chrysostom's *Trojan Oration* in his important book on the Second Sophistic: "the ultimate extravagance of *anaskeuê*" (*The Second Sophistic: A Cultural Phenomenon in the Roman Empire* [London: Routledge, 1993], 50). On the Gnostic side, see Michael Williams's critique of value-laden scholarly misconstruals of Gnostic biblical interpretation in *Rethinking "Gnosticism": An Argument for Dismantling a Dubious Category* (Princeton: Princeton University Press, 1996), 68–72.

Elijah-Elisha cycle from 1–2 Kings that MacDonald claims Mark adopts toward Homeric epic—an analogous emulation of supremely authoritative sacred literature by means of which Jesus is assimilated to and distinguished from legendary scriptural heroes.[66]

The characteristic response to MacDonald's scholarship on Homer and the Gospels has been to "go small," to question the validity of the Homeric allusions he observes or to proliferate criteria necessary to determine the presence of literary allusions or echoes.[67] I am not unsympathetic to such criticism of his work, and I confess to not always being convinced by his intertextual readings. However, what his provocative scholarship ultimately calls for is not ever more nuanced debate about what does or does not constitute a valid literary allusion in an ancient text, but rather broad recognition that the scriptural scene of the Roman imperial world in which the Gospels were composed differs more fundamentally from that of the contemporary Western world than New Testament scholars regularly acknowledge. To a large extent, in the Roman imperial world, ancient Jewish, Christian, and pagan intellectuals (and I recognize the problems with every one of those terms) shared the same culturally authoritative texts. Some tended to value particular texts more than others, but these judgments were often relative, rather than absolute. The pagan philosopher Numenius, for instance, can cite Moses as a scriptural authority alongside Homer (Fr. 30 Des Places), while Mark

---

[66] Winn, *Mark and the Elijah-Elisha Narrative*.

[67] For a typical review, see Morna D. Hooker, review of *The Homeric Epics and the Gospel of Mark*, by Dennis R. MacDonald, *JTS* 53.1 (2002): 196–98. For a more sophisticated but equally negative assessment, see Karl Olav Sandnes, "*Imitatio Homeri*? An Appraisal of Dennis R. MacDonald's 'Mimesis Criticism,'" *JBL* 124.4 (2005): 715–32. A similar, cautionary call for criteria may also be found in the initial chapter of this volume: Mark G. Bilby, "Mainstreaming Mimesis Criticism," *supra*.

can subtly invoke Homer while explicitly engaging with the Septuagint.[68] One might infer that Mark privileges the scriptural authority of the Bible over that of Homer, but even that relatively uncontroversial inference must be complicated, for Mark may keep Homeric epic at a distance—subtly alluding to it rather than quoting it outright—but he never subjects Homer to the kind of subversive critique he levels at Moses, as in chapter 10, where he asserts that Mosaic law distorts God's will for political purposes. Beyond the fact that they interpreted a common body of scriptural writings, diverse ancient writers had available to them a shared collection of conventional hermeneutical approaches on which they drew to rewrite and interpret texts granted supreme cultural and religious authority—Homer and the Bible especially.

The ancient scriptural scene, MacDonald's work suggests, is larger and far more complex than many New Testament scholars have assumed. The true challenge of his scholarship is not to reimagine or resist reimagining one or another episode in Mark, or Mark's Gospel in its entirety (the first two-thirds of this essay notwithstanding), or even the entire synoptic tradition (although MacDonald himself has recently pushed his work in this direction).[69] It is rather to develop and apply to Roman imperial literature broadly conceived a coherent and persuasive concept of authoritative scripture, and to try to understand the complex but still recognizable patterns of response ancient Mediterranean writers from disparate religious traditions display when they interpret and revise various religiously and culturally

---

[68] Numenius, *Fragments* (ed. Édouard des Places; Paris: Les Belles Lettres, 2003), 80–81.

[69] See Dennis R. MacDonald, *Two Shipwrecked Gospels: The* Logoi *of Jesus and Papias's* Exposition of Logia about the Lord (ECL 8; Atlanta: Society of Biblical Literature, 2012).

authoritative texts in the context of their own literary and ideological pursuits.

Acts 2 as an Intertextual Map: Moving from Dionysian to Platonic Identity
Ilseo Park

Acts 2 as Programmatic Chapter: Argument and Scholarship

There is no doubt that the author of Acts not only collected and redacted sources for his work, but also rewrote the Hebrew Bible-LXX and imitated the famous Greco-Roman classics in his writing. While historical critical scholarship has stressed the former feature of Acts, literary critics have focused on the latter, the literary aspect of Acts. They have attempted to identify the author's models to which his work alluded and to investigate his compositional competency by comparing classical literature and employing various literary-critical methods. Accordingly, scholarly debates on the genre of Acts have become more invigorated than ever, though a consensus has not been reached.[1] These vibrant discussions about the genre and the theological ends of Acts in a way reflect the author's proficiency and sophistication, as well as the contribution of literary-critical readings to Acts scholarship. Starting with the assumption of Acts as the product of an author more than a collector, this presentation will focus on one literary strategy, mimesis, as found in Acts 2. It will show that Acts 2 is a programmatic chapter not only from theological and narrative perspectives, but also in terms of the mimetic intertextuality of the entire corpus of Acts.

It is not new to say that Acts 2 is a programmatic chapter or prolepsis for the rest of Acts. Scholarly attention

---

[1] See, e.g., Thomas E. Phillips, "The Genre of Acts: Moving toward a Consensus?" *CBR* 4.3 (2006): 361–94.

focuses on the outpouring of the Spirit upon the disciples, which represents the beginning of the church and brings about miraculous speaking in tongues and the capacity of people from many nations to comprehend. For commentators, the list of nations (Acts 2:9–11) demonstrates the universal nature of Christian teaching and the legitimacy of the Gentile mission. The geographical distribution in the list reaffirms Acts 1:8 and at the same time anticipates the expansion of the Christian mission to Rome in chapter 28. Gary Gilbert argues for the universalism of the list by comparing it with Roman propagandistic literature.[2] In this reading, the list anticipates the successful mission of early Christianity to the Gentiles just as Roman rule expanded over neighboring countries. Some scholars note that the Pentecost episode reveals a reversal of the Babel story (Gen 11:1–9). For example, Craig Keener mentions that "in Genesis, God descended and scattered tongues to prevent unity; in Acts, the Spirit descends and scatters tongues to create multicultural unity."[3] With little variation, almost all their claims are about the author's universalism as related to early Christian faith and community.

    The quotation of Joel that immediately follows is also cited as evidence of universalism, in that this eschatological outpouring of the Spirit overcomes ethnic, class, gender, and age barriers. Indeed, God's Spirit will come upon "all flesh" (Joel 2:28, [3:1 LXX]). Huub van de Sandt convincingly demonstrates that Luke's rewriting of Joel's prophecy in Acts 2 transformed the tenor of Joel, which held, in its original context, that on the last day Jews would gather in Jerusalem to

---

[2] Gary Gilbert, "The List of Nations in Acts 2: Roman Ideology and the Lucan Response," *JBL* 121.3 (2002): 497–529.

[3] Craig S. Keener, *Acts: An Exegetical Commentary* (4 vols.; Grand Rapids: Baker Academic, 2012–2015), 1:843.

repent and that the Gentiles would fight against God.[4] According to his theological program, Luke attempts to transform this pattern. Rather than a movement from scattering to eschatological gathering, this one traces the eschatological gathering of Jews and Gentiles together, leading to a scattering for mission. The outpouring of the Holy Spirit as an eschatological phenomenon between the Pentecost event and the one in Joel makes this link plausible and triggers this interpretation.

It is the Christian community that can carry out the mission to the Gentiles on the basis of its universal perspective. The formation of this community in Acts 2:42–47 is described in an idealistic manner. Prior to its process of maturation, the community demonstrates a utopian quality: the sharing of possessions. Such an extremely idealistic portrayal of communalism has led even scholars who read Acts as historical to raise doubts about its historicity here. For example, F. F. Bruce concluded that this idealized portrayal of the primitive church has no historical basis.[5] On the literary level, however, the author's portrayal of the nascent Christian community clearly reveals the church as an eschatological event, "a miracle" fulfilling the promise of Deuteronomy, the teachings of Jesus, and the ideals of Greek utopianism. Thus, in Acts, the early church is no doubt the right and the only institution to carry out the mission to the Gentiles with a truly universal vision.

In sum, traditional readings of Acts 2 mainly stress the universal vision revealed in the Pentecost event, along with the proleptic geographical expansion and the formation of church as an eschatological miracle, as well as its function for

---

[4] Huub van de Sandt, "The Fate of the Gentiles in Joel and Acts 2: An Intertextual Study," *ETL* 66.1 (1990): 56–77, here 58.

[5] F. F. Bruce, *The Book of the Acts* (rev. ed.; NICNT; Grand Rapids: Eerdmans, 1988), 72–75.

the rest of the narrative. Accordingly, on the narrative level, this chapter has rightly been suggested as an outline of the Lukan program foreshadowing the subsequent narratives in Acts.

Mimetic Intertextuality in Acts 2

Acts 2 is also a programmatic chapter in terms of mimetic intertextuality. It has been well attested that Acts has much in common with the *Bacchae*.[6] For example, some suggest that the list of nations is comparable to the list in the *Bacchae*, in which Dionysus the protagonist boastfully enumerates the list of nations to which he introduced the rites.[7] Additionally, the references to wine, the spirit as a liquid, and charge of drunkenness make this literary connection more plausible. It should be remembered that, next to Homer, Euripides was the most frequently learned and read text for the primary stage of education in antiquity.[8] The *Bacchae* and other Dionysiac myths frequently serve as literary models and pools of motifs to imitate because of their universal tenor, suspenseful tragic plot, and other motifs. In keeping with the development of Hellenistic cosmopolitanism, the universal inclusiveness of Dionysiac tradition appealed to the ruling class. They often identified themselves as the "new Dionysus."

In addition, the popularity of Dionysiac mystery religions in the Mediterranean milieu also heightens the possibility of the conscious usage of Dionysiac motifs. For

---

[6] In this volume, see Michael Kochenash, "The Scandal of Gentile Inclusion: Reading Acts 17 with Euripides' *Bacchae*," *infra*. Note 3 of that chapter gives a helpful list of the history of scholarship.

[7] Dennis R. MacDonald, *Luke and Vergil: Imitations of Classical Greek Literature* (NTGL 2; Lanham, MD: Rowman & Littlefield, 2015), 25.

[8] See, e.g., Teresa Morgan, *Literate Education in the Hellenistic and Roman Worlds* (Cambridge: Cambridge University Press, 1998), 59, 69–72, 115–16.

incipient Christianity, which had to characterize and propagandize itself to outsiders, Dionysiac religion was likely the optimal religious tradition among those available that early Christians could adopt for their missional purpose. The positive quality of the universal appeal of Dionysus, the plot of the introduction of his cult into a new soil in the *Bacchae*, and the popularity of the mystery religions were all attractive, especially for a writing such as Acts which narrates the Christian mission to "the end of the earth" (Acts 1:8).

Despite these aforementioned positive qualities, however, Dionysiac rites were often suspected for immoral behaviors such as secret nocturnal rites, the illicit comingling of men and women, drunkenness, and irrational frenzy. Senatorial legislation on the Bacchanalia in 186 BCE illustrates the perception of this religion at that time, however overstated in tone. Regarding this matter, Courtney Friesen notes the similar charges against Christians in Bithynia of Pliny the Younger (*Ep.* 10.96).[9] Following Robert M. Grant's lead, he argues that Pliny's description of Christians was shaped by Livy's account of Bacchanalia and that at least one of the historical figures perceived Christianity in light of Dionysiac religion.[10] What matters in the given topic is that borrowing even positive qualities as literary motifs from Dionysiac tradition entails the risk of charges such as immorality and irrational ritual acts. This is the point where the apologetic concern of Acts enters.

The Pentecost event reflects the universal vision of Christianity and anticipates the expansion of the Christian mission in the rest of narrative. Evoking Dionysiac motifs,

---

[9] Courtney J. P. Friesen, *Reading Dionysus: Euripides'* Bacchae *and the Cultural Contestations of Greeks, Jews, Romans, and Christians* (STAC 95; Tübingen: Mohr Siebeck, 2015), 22–23.

[10] See Robert M. Grant, "Pliny and the Christians," *HTR* 41.4 (1948): 273–74.

here specifically the *Bacchae*, the author of Acts successfully demonstrates the universalism of Christian teaching. However, his literary exploits do not end here. In keeping with this Bacchic emphasis on universalism, he attempts to draw the attention of readers to prophecy in the form of glossolalia, which is unexpectedly intelligible to people from various cultural and linguistic backgrounds. While in the narrative people ridicule the apostles' prophecy as a drunken murmuring, the narrative repeatedly insists on its intelligibility (Acts 2:8, 11).

The association of drunkenness and prophecy and misperception of ritual drinking as debauchery appear also in the *Bacchae*. In *Bacch*. 221–22, Pentheus accuses the maenads of drunkenness of wine, which leads to dancing and licentiousness: "they [maenads] set up full wine bowls in the middle of their assemblies and sneak off, one here, one there to tryst in private with men." Against this charge, in *Bacch*. 298–301, Tiresias defends Dionysus before Pentheus saying "this god is also a prophet [μάντις]. For the ecstatic/Baachic [τό βακχεύσιμον] and the manic [τό μανιῶδες] have mantic [μαντικήν] powers in large measure. When the god enters someone in force, he causes him in madness [μεμηνόντας] to predict the future." This remark reveals ritual wine drinking and seemingly consequent drunkenness as a legitimate means of divine inspiration to prophecy. In this regard, it is worth noting that Philo also points out that divine madness, notably using the cognate Greek word, βεβάκχευται, was necessary for prophecy and that it could be seen as drunkenness or madness to the unenlightened (*Ebr.* 146). Thus, just as Tiresias notes drunkenness or madness as a means of prophecy, Acts attempts to defend the Spirit-led speaking in tongues within the early church, that while it sounds like drunken, unintelligible glossolalia to outsiders, it is actually intelligible prophecy.

To highlight the rationality of Christianity and debunk the accusation of drunkenness, Acts also adds the quotation of Joel's prophecy that grounds speaking in tongues as both a fulfillment of the Jewish prophets and as an understandable speech act. Moreover, Acts carefully adds "they shall prophesy" (2:18), which is not in the original text, to the quotation of Joel 2:28–32. In this way, the apologetic rationality of Christians grows in concert with their distance from negative Dionysiac accusations.

But what is the ultimate symbol of rationality? Philosophical teaching and practice. As stated above, scholars note that the promises of Deuteronomy, Jesus's teachings, and Greek utopianism are echoed in Luke's description of the Christian community in the summary section in Acts 2:42–47. However, in terms of intertextuality, Rubén Dupertuis convincingly argues that the summaries in Acts 2, 4, and 5 reflect direct literary indebtedness to Plato's writing, especially the *Republic*.[11] He posits that it is inevitable that Luke was likely exposed to several works of Plato in light of the relatively high level of education indicated by Luke's literary style and language. He also explores the prevailing utopian tradition in antiquity and asserts that Plato's works made a considerable impact on the development of this tradition. At their early stage, the utopian traditions were largely based on mythological utopias found in Homer and Hesiod. However, after Plato, the utopian traditions were dominated by the reason and rationality that Plato proposed in the *Republic*, including the stress on the sharing of possessions. In Acts the representative feature of the early community is also depicted as the sharing of possessions. Lexical parallels between Plato and Acts such as κοινωνία

---

[11] Rubén R. Dupertuis, "The Summaries in Acts 2, 4 and 5 and Greek Utopian Literary Traditions" (PhD diss., Claremont Graduate University, 2005), 81.

(2:42), ἐπὶ τὸ αὐτο (2:44, 47), καρδία καὶ ψυχὴ μία (4:32) all point to direct literary dependence.

In Plato's work, this communalism is achieved only by the guardians, the so-called philosopher-kings. That is to say, the practice of ultimate rationality engenders utopian community. By evoking Plato's utopia, Acts 2 claims that the Christian community achieves the ideal of philosophers and realizes the golden age here and now, which had never been accomplished in human history, even by the Greeks. In this regard, Acts asserts not only that Christianity is a philosophical community, but also that it is superior to Greek philosophical tradition and rationality. The latter is a very bold claim, considering the high status of Greek culture in the Roman empire.

As seen above, Acts 2 begins with allusions to the *Bacchae* as a demonstration of the universal nature of Christianity. Against pejorative charges of drunkenness and debauchery (Acts 2:13), the author alludes to the association between drunkenness and the act of Dionysiac prophecy, while repeatedly drawing attention to the issue of intelligibility. The quotation of Joel and its expansion strengthens the conception of speaking in tongues as an intelligible prophecy. Consequently, it distances Christians from the public misconception of them as immoral Dionysiac followers, just as Pliny the Younger had depicted them. Furthermore, by describing the first Christian community with Platonic utopian language, Luke characterizes Christians as a group of philosophers that realizes the Greco-Roman ideal of the sharing of all things.

While frequently alluding to the Septuagint, the entire structure of Acts enacts a sustained transition from Dionysiac tradition to Plato's works and repeatedly brings rationality into focus. This constant emphasis on rationality responds to outsider understandings of Christians. As in Pliny's charge against Christians as part of a "depraved and excessive superstition" (*Ep.* 10.96), the early church encountered pejorative remarks about their faith as irrational and incompatible with philosophy. Early Christian theologians such as Origen and Justin Martyr, therefore, had to defend the compatibility of Christian faith with rationality (Origen, *Cels.*, I.9; Justin, *Dial.*, 8.1). The literary project of Acts was likely related to the early church's actual struggle to define the Christian faith as rational and philosophical. To achieve this apologetic goal, on the one hand, Acts imitates the *Bacchae* because of its popularity and similarity with Christian teaching, while still retaining a focus on rationality. On the other hand, by imitating Plato Acts affirms that Christianity is philosophical, even more than Greek philosophy itself.

The distribution of antetexts is notable. The imitations and allusions to the *Bacchae* cluster in the first half of Acts, while the imitations of Plato's work cluster in the second half. In his recent book, *Luke and Vergil*, MacDonald provides the list of antetexts imitated in each chapter of Acts.[12] Chapter 17 falls approximately in the middle of Acts. Here Paul enters Athens, the city of philosophers (17:15). His description of Athens—"the city was full of idols" (17:16)—corresponds to the way the detractors of Christianity described it as a superstition adhered to by irrational maniacs. In spite of their philosophical pedigree, the Athenians do not perceive the true god who "is not far from each one" (17:27). They are like Pentheus in the *Bacchae,* who does not recognize Dionysus even when he is near him. Also, in the same way Pentheus ridicules the deity, some Athenians scoff at Paul's teaching about the true God (17:32a).

In these allusions to the *Bacchae*, what is most notable is the characterization of Paul. He is depicted as legendary philosopher, a new Socrates. Karl Olav Sandnes notes that

---

[12] MacDonald, *Luke and Vergil*, 121–22.

Paul's speech in Areopagus adopts the same rhetorical device Socrates used in the *Apology*: *insinuatio*.[13] Moreover, he lists several parallels with Socratic traditions. David M. Reis and MacDonald go further and argue that Acts does not simply borrow generic Socratic motifs, but instead imitates Plato's work to depict Paul as Christian Socrates.[14] According to Reis and MacDonald, by so doing, Acts attempts to defend Christianity's commitment to reason by "Paulinizing" Socrates, which invites the reader to identify Paul as a Christian Socrates. The emphasis of Acts on the rationality of Christianity becomes more prominent and obvious after Acts 17 in its repeated portrayal of Paul as a new, superior Socrates.[15]

Conclusion

Acts 2 is rightly affirmed as a programmatic chapter in terms of its theological perspective and narrative development because it outlines a forthcoming geographical expansion, the role of the Holy Spirit and the Christian community in the mission to the Gentiles. The programmatic role of this chapter also pertains to its intertextual strategy. The sequential pattern of the imitation of the *Bacchae* and Plato that first appear in Acts 2 extends into the entire structure of Acts: the *Bacchae* in

---

[13] Karl Olav Sandnes, "Paul and Socrates: The Aim of Paul's Areopagus Speech," *JSNT* 15.50 (1993): 21.

[14] David M. Reis, "The Areopagus as Echo Chamber: *Mimesis* and Intertextuality in Acts," *JHC* 9.2 (2002): 272-73 and MacDonald, *Luke and Vergil*, 76–81.

[15] See also Rubén R. Dupertuis, "Bold Speech, Opposition, and Philosophical Imagery in Acts," *Engaging Early Christian History: Reading Acts in the Second Century* (ed. Rubén R. Dupertuis and Todd Penner; London: Routledge, 2014), 153–68 and Ryan Carhart, "The Second Sophistic and the Cultural Idealization of Paul in Acts," *Engaging Early Christian History: Reading Acts in the Second Century* (ed. Rubén R. Dupertuis and Todd Penner; London: Routledge, 2014), 187–208.

the first half and Plato the second half. In addition, just as in Acts 2, the emphasis on the rationality of Christianity is strengthened by the transition of antetexts from Bacchic to Platonic as the narrative unfolds across the remainder of Acts. Chapter 17 works as a pivot by describing the Athenian failure to comprehend the true god and by illustrating the superiority of Christian rationality to Athenian philosophy via Paul, the Christian Socrates. This theme persists and re-emerges until the closure of the book in chapter 28. Thus, Acts 2 provides a mimetic microcosm of the entire world of Acts.

The Scandal of Gentile Inclusion: Reading Acts 17 with Euripides' Bacchae
Michael Kochenash

A Dionysian Pattern in the Acts of the Apostles

Euripides' tragic play the *Bacchae* was written the same year the playwright died, near the end of the fifth century BCE. It was first performed after his death at the Athenian Theater of Dionysus, on the Acropolis, during the spring festival honoring Dionysus in 401 BCE. The tragic storyline driving the narrative centers on Dionysus's divine conception—he was fathered by Zeus—and the revenge he exacts upon his unbelieving cousin and aunts. The narrative framework within which this tragedy unfolds is most relevant here: Dionysus introducing his cult to the inhabitants of Thebes. In the *Bacchae*, the king of Thebes becomes anxious on account of the popularity of this newly arrived religious movement from the east (Asia Minor), especially among the leading women of the city, including the king's female kin—his mother and aunts. A scandal becomes attached to the Dionysian movement due to suggestions of sexual impropriety. As a result, Pentheus—the king and also Dionysus's cousin—persecutes the priest of the Dionysian cult, who is in fact Dionysus in disguise. The tragedy ends with Dionysus inducing the Theban bacchants—including Pentheus's female kin—into a frenzy, wherein they dismember the king. Pentheus's mother herself parades his decapitated head, mounted on a thyrsus, into Thebes.

Although considerably less graphic, there are certain narratives in the Acts of the Apostles that reflect this Euripidean plot structure. Two such narratives occur at the beginning of Acts 17. In the first narrative (Acts 17:1–9), Paul arrives in Thessalonica and wins a following that consists of some Jews from the synagogue along with "many of the devout Greeks and not a few of the leading women" (17:4). The unconvinced Jews become anxious, form a mob, and enlist the aid of the city authorities in their opposition to Paul. In the next scene (17:10-15), Paul and Silas escape to Beroea. The Jews there are presented as more receptive to Paul than those in Thessalonica. "Many of them" believed, "including not a few prominent Greek women and men" (17:12). The anxious Jews from Thessalonica reappear in Beroea, however, and again stir up trouble. Again Paul escapes.

A dominant narrative concern in both Luke and Acts is the articulation of a particular vision of the kingdom of God.[1] Amid Luke's narrations of this theme, one potentially troublesome subplot frequently surfaces: though Christianity is a Jewish movement, many Jews reject it.[2] The Thessalonian and Beroean narratives in Acts 17 foreground this subplot. In this chapter, I read the two narrative episodes in Acts 17:1-15 as imitating Euripides' *Bacchae* and explore how this reading can be interpreted as addressing the dilemma of certain Jews rejecting Paul's proclamation.[3]

---

[1] See Christian Blumenthal, *Basileia bei Lukas: Studien zur erzählerischen Entfaltung der lukanischen Basileiakonzeption* (HBS 84; Freiburg: Herder, 2016).

[2] E.g., Luke 2:28-35; 4:16-30; 13:22-30; 14:12-24; 19:1-10; Acts 10:1-11:18; 21:27-31.

[3] For the use of Euripides' *Bacchae* in Luke and/or Acts, see Wilhelm Nestle, "Anklänge an Euripides in der Apostelgeschichte," *Phil* 59 (1900): 46-57; Friedrich Smend, "Untersuchungen zu den Acta-Darstellungen von der Bekehrung des Paulus," *Angelos* 1 (1925): 34-45; Otto Weinreich, *Gebet und Wunder: Zwei Abhandlungen zur Religions- und Literaturgeschichte in Religionsgeschichtliche Studien* (Darmstadt: Wissenschaftliche Buchgesellschaft, 1968), 1-198; Detlef Ziegler, *Dionysos in der Apostelgeschichte – eine intertextuelle Lektüre* (Religion und Biographie 18; Berlin: Lit, 2008); Dennis R. MacDonald, "Classical Greek Poetry and the Acts of the Apostles: Imitations of Euripides' *Bacchae*," *Christian Origins*

Jason in Thessalonica, Jason in Thessaly

The Thessalonian narrative in Acts divides neatly into two parts: the proclamation of Paul and Silas (Acts 17:1-4) and the aggressive opposition of certain Jews to their message (17:5-9).[4] As I explain in greater detail in a later section, the first part follows the Euripidean narrative structure outlined above. The second part reinforces the Euripidean theme of anxiety—exhibited here as anxiety regarding the identity of those gaining inclusion into the Christian movement—but then transitions into an Argonaut motif.

Although previously focused on Paul and Silas, the narrative shifts the readers' attention to Jason in 17:5b. No explanation is given for his identity, suggesting that the

---

and Greco-Roman Culture: Social and Literary Contexts for the New Testament (ed. Stanley E. Porter and Andrew W. Pitts; ECHC 1; TENTS 9; Leiden: Brill 2013), 463-96; Dennis R. MacDonald, *Luke and Vergil: Imitations of Classical Greek Literature* (NTGL 2; Lanham, MD: Rowman & Littlefield, 2015), 11-65; Courtney J. P. Friesen, *Reading Dionysus: Euripides'* Bacchae *and the Cultural Contestations of Greeks, Jews, Romans, and Christians* (STAC 95; Tübingen: Mohr Siebeck, 2015), 207-35; Harold W. Attridge, "Paul and Pentheus: What's in a Possible Allusion," *Delightful Acts: New Essays on Canonical and Non-Canonical Acts* (ed. Harold W. Attridge, Dennis R. MacDonald, and Clare K. Rothschild; WUNT I/391; Tübingen: Mohr Siebeck, 2017), 7-18; and Ilseo Park, "Acts 2 as an Intertextual Map: Moving from Dionysian to Platonic Identity," *supra*. Other scholars reject the idea of Luke's direct literary dependence on the *Bacchae*, including: Alfred Vögeli, "Lukas und Euripides," *TZ* 9 (1953): 415-38; Reinhard Kratz, *Rettungswunder: Motiv-, traditions- und formkritische Aufarbeitung einer biblischen Gattung* (EH 23/123; Frankfurt am Main: Peter Lang, 1979); Richard Seaford, "Thunder, Lightning and Earthquake in the *Bacchae* and the Acts of the Apostles," *What Is a God? Studies in the Nature of Greek Divinity* (ed. Alan B. Lloyd; London: Duckworth, 1997), 139-52; and John B. Weaver, *Plots of Epiphany: Prison Escape in the Acts of the Apostles* (BZNW 131; Berlin: de Gruyter, 2004).

[4] The opposition can be characterized as "aggressive" on the basis of the verbs used: becoming jealous (17:5), forming a mob (17:5), creating an uproar (17:5), attacking Jason's house (17:5), dragging Jason (17:6), and shouting (17:6).

implied audience either knows who he is or understands the significance of his name.⁵ Accordingly, scholars often attribute the narrative featuring Jason (17:5b–9) to a tradition of some sort, but as Richard I. Pervo observes, "Acceptance of this source adds nothing to the understanding of the passage, since Jason makes no meaningful contribution."⁶ Dennis R. MacDonald argues compellingly, however, that Jason's *name* does make a meaningful contribution to the Acts narrative.

Jason was a famous mythological figure, perhaps most well-known from Euripides' *Medea* and the *Argonautica* by Apollonius of Rhodes. In *Luke and Vergil: Imitations of Classical Greek Literature*, MacDonald compares the Thessalonian narrative in Acts with the fourth *Pythian Ode* by Pindar, featuring Jason and the Golden Fleece.⁷ The most salient parallels that Acts shares with the Jason myth, however, are not specific to any one of its iterations, including Pindar's. Accordingly, it may be more credible to read the Thessalonian narrative in Acts instead alongside the distinctive elements

---

⁵ Similarly, Craig S. Keener: "Luke mentions Jason as if he were already known, perhaps because Luke may write for a partly Macedonian audience or perhaps because he has again condensed material overzealously" (*Acts: An Exegetical Commentary* [4 vol.; Grand Rapids: Baker Academic, 2012–2015], 3:2549). MacDonald notes, "Rom 16:21 mentions a Jason who was with Paul in Corinth, but no person with this name appears in Macedonia apart from Acts" (*Luke and Vergil*, 49). The suggestion that the Jason in Acts 17 ought to be identified with the Jason in Rom 16 is thus not credible.

⁶ Richard I. Pervo, *Acts: A Commentary* (ed. Harold W. Attridge; Hermeneia; Minneapolis: Fortress, 2009), 418. On the attribution of the name Jason to tradition, see, e.g., C. K. Barrett: "The name Jason suggests contact with local tradition" (*A Critical and Exegetical Commentary on the Acts of the Apostles* [2 vol.; ICC 34; Edinburgh: T&T Clark, 1994–1998], 2:807).

⁷ MacDonald, *Luke and Vergil*, 48–50. Keener is among the commentators who explicitly reject a connection with Jason of the Argonauts (*Acts*, 3:2550).

that are commonly reproduced in ancient literature narrating the Jason myth.

The story of Jason and the Golden Fleece begins with Pelias, the king of Iolcus in Thessaly, receiving a warning—sometimes described as coming from an oracle—about a threat to his kingship.[8] According to Apollonius of Rhodes, Pelias learns that he will "perish through the designs of that man whom he would see coming from the people with only one sandal" (*Argon.* 1.6-7 [Race, LCL]). Similar narrative preambles appear, for example, in Pindar, *Pyth.* 4.71-78 and Valerius Flaccus, *Argon.* 1.26-30. Sure enough, Jason soon arrives with only one sandal, and Pelias rightly regards one-sandaled Jason as a threat to the throne. The Iolcian king thus arranges to dispatch Jason in search of the Golden Fleece, a mission that Pelias knows will be perilous. Pindar explains that Pelias offered to relinquish the throne of Iolcus—which Pelias had taken, unjustly, from his half-brother Aeson, Jason's father—upon Jason's return following his completion of this task (*Pyth.* 4.156-68). Pelias, of course, expects that Jason will die in the pursuit of the fleece, in which case he would not need to honor his commitment to abdicate. Nevertheless, Jason—accompanied by a band of heroic figures, including Heracles—sets out in search of the Golden Fleece aboard their ship, the *Argo*. Thus begin the adventures of Jason and the Argonauts. The salient features of the beginning of the Jason myth, as far as it pertains to the Thessalonian narrative in Acts, thus include a man named Jason, a threat to the ruling order, a reactive attempt to protect the ruling order, and a group of companions.

The unexplained inclusion of the name Jason in the Thessalonian narrative prompts readers to consider whether

---

[8] For this introduction to the Jason myth, see, e.g., Pindar, *Pyth.* 4.71-119; Apollonius of Rhodes, *Argon.* 1.5-17; and Valerius Flaccus, *Argon.* 1.22-63.

other elements might correspond to the mythology surrounding Jason, son of Aeson. Indeed, MacDonald identifies elements corresponding to each of the salient features outlined in the previous paragraph.[9] In addition to the inclusion of a man named Jason and "etymologically similar home regions [Thessaly and Thessalonica], both of which are in northeastern Greece," the Thessalonian narrative in Acts is animated in particular by an apparent threat to the ruling order and its subsequent suppression.[10] In response to Paul's proclamation of Jesus as the Messiah who needed "to suffer and to rise from the dead" (Acts 17:2-3), certain unconvinced Jewish listeners report this activity to the civic rulers as "acting contrary to the decrees of Caesar, saying there is another emperor, Jesus" (17:7). The reasoning underlying this accusation appears to rely on the association of Jesus as the Messiah with the ancient Jewish anticipation of the Davidic monarchy's restoration. Nevertheless, the actual cause of their opposition to Paul, according to the narrator, is jealousy (17:5). These Jewish opponents assemble a mob in order to apprehend Paul and Silas and attack Jason's house — the first time Jason is mentioned in the narrative. With Paul and Silas nowhere to be found, they elect to apprehend Jason along with his comrades (17:6) — analogues to Jason's Argonauts — and bring them before the civic assembly where they raise the charges of sedition quoted above (17:7).

Remarkably, the D-text of Acts 17:15 adds that Paul "passed by Thessaly, for he was prevented from proclaiming the message to them."[11] Although it would, of course, be impossible to confirm, this insertion may indicate that the scribe observed the Argonaut parallels and wanted to explain why Paul avoids the region traditionally associated with

---

[9] See MacDonald, *Luke and Vergil*, 49.
[10] MacDonald, *Luke and Vergil*, 49.
[11] For the content of the D-text, see, e.g., Pervo, *Acts*.

Jason—employing language reminiscent of Acts 16:7. If so, the implied D-text reader might imagine that a scenario exhibiting the features that Acts 17:1–9 shares with the Jason myth awaited Paul yet again in Thessaly, and so he was prevented from going there.[12]

Be that as it may, the narrative's introduction of an otherwise unknown character named Jason—for readers with the appropriate cultural competence—evokes the theme of threats to the ruling order, made explicit in Acts 17:7. Nevertheless, the invocation of the name Jason is ironic. The supposed political threat posed by Paul, Silas, Jason, and the other believers is undermined by the unreliability of the characters accusing them of sedition—they are motivated only by jealousy. The name Jason thus evokes the idea of a threat to the ruling order, an idea that appears to reinforce the accusations of Paul's opponents but which is emphatically undermined by the narrative's specification of their motive. This use of the Jason myth is situated within a narrative structure that imitates the plot of Euripides' *Bacchae*, which can be read as an explanatory frame of reference for interpreting the Jewish rejection of the followers of Jesus.

Frames of Reference for Jewish Rejection

The first part of the Thessalonian narrative begins with Paul arriving and promptly visiting the local synagogue, "as was his custom [κατὰ . . . τὸ εἰωθὸς]," where he "argued with them from the scriptures" (Acts 17:1–2). An identical phrase appears in Luke 4:16 when Jesus goes to the synagogue on the Sabbath, "as was his custom [κατὰ . . . τὸ εἰωθὸς]."[13] This verb

---

[12] Alternatively, the scribe may have wanted to anticipate Paul's Socratic characterization in Athens. See MacDonald, *Luke and Vergil*, 90–94.

[13] See Keener, *Acts*, 3:2541. Paul often goes to the synagogue in Acts (13:5, 14; 14:1; 17:10, 17; 18:4, 19; 19:8), but Luke nowhere else describes it as Paul's custom.

(ἔθω) appears only twice elsewhere in the New Testament (Matt 27:15; Mark 10:1).[14] The connection of this phrase with the circumstance of discussing scripture in a synagogue in both Luke 4 and Acts 17 is suggestive. Readers who correlate Acts 17:1-2 with Luke 4:16 might thus interpret the Thessalonian narrative by reference to Luke 4:16-30 and the theme of opposition to Jesus's vision for the kingdom of God.

In Luke 4, Jesus reads from Isaiah and identifies himself as the fulfillment of its prophecies concerning the restoration of Israel (Luke 4:16-21). At the conclusion of this episode, those in the synagogue attempt to end Jesus's life by throwing him off a cliff.[15] Their outrage is sparked by Jesus's citation of Biblical narratives wherein Elijah and Elisha share God's benefactions with religious and ethnic outsiders (4:25-30). The kingdom of God inaugurated by Jesus in Luke 4 emphasizes the distribution of God's benefactions outside the Jewish religious and social center.[16] Much like Paul in Acts 17, Jesus is rejected by some of his Jewish listeners. In Luke 4, as elsewhere in the Third Gospel, the author explains the Jewish rejection of Jesus by reference to the Israelite rejection of Hebrew prophets. Jesus is thus aligned with Elijah and Elisha, proleptically exemplifying his later statement in the Sermon on the Plain: "Blessed are you when people hate you, and when they exclude you, revile you, and defame you . . . for that is what their ancestors did to the prophets" (Luke 6:22-23). Those who interpret Jesus's rejection by certain Jews within this prophetic framework might thus have their

---

[14] Matthew 27:15 refers to Pilate releasing a prisoner; Mark 10:1 refers to Jesus teaching crowds that had gathered around him.

[15] For the significance of the cliff, see Margaret Froelich and Thomas E. Phillips, "Throw the Blasphemer off a Cliff: Luke 4.16-30 in Light of the *Life of Aesop*," *NTS*, forthcoming.

[16] See Michael Kochenash, "Empire without End: Juxtaposing the Kingdom of God with Rome in Luke-Acts" (PhD diss., Claremont School of Theology, 2017), 94–116, especially 103–09.

anxieties assuaged. Far from discrediting Jesus and his followers, such rejection serves to validate their prophetic status by associating them with the Biblical Hebrew prophets.

The narrative of Acts 17:1-9 can be read as addressing this same anxiety, establishing an additional frame of reference for understanding the rejection of Jesus and his followers: the plot of Euripides' *Bacchae*. Specifically, three elements of the Thessalonian narrative appear to imitate the plot of the *Bacchae*: (1) the promulgation of a religious movement that came to a Greek region from across the Aegean Sea; (2) the remarkable success of that religious movement among prominent women; and (3) the consequent anxiety regarding the success of that religious movement, even involving city authorities.

The Philippian Narrative as Context for the Thessalonian Narrative

In Acts 16:11-12, Paul and his companions—narrated in the first-person plural—sail from Troas in Asia Minor to the province of Macedonia, specifically to the Roman colony of Philippi. Paul's trans-Aegean route, of course, recalls those of Odysseus in Homer's *Odyssey* and Aeneas in Virgil's *Aeneid*, the latter imitating the former.[17] More generally, however, the trans-Aegean movement also recalls the premise of the *Bacchae*: Dionysus came to Thebes from Asia Minor. In the prologue, Dionysus claims, "I have come to this land of Thebes as the son of Zeus. Dionysus is my name" (*Bacch.* 1-2; see also 13-42).[18] Later, he addresses the bacchants who came with him, "Hail, my sisterhood of worshippers, you who left Mt. Tmolus, bulwark of Lydia, women I wooed from foreign

---

[17] See, e.g., Dennis R. MacDonald, *The Gospels and Homer: Imitations of Greek Epic in Mark and Luke-Acts* (NTGL 1; Lanham, MD: Rowman & Littlefield, 2015), 191-93 and MacDonald, *Luke and Vergil*, 153-55.

[18] All translations from the *Bacchae* are taken from Stephen Esposito, *Euripides' Bacchae: Translation, Introduction, and Notes* (Focus Classical Library; Newburyport, MA: Focus, 1998).

lands" (55-56). Lydia and Mt. Tmolus are, of course, located in western Asia Minor. Considered in isolation, these parallels between Paul's and Dionysus's trans-Aegean movements are unremarkable. When reconsidered in light of the striking parallels that follow in Acts 16, however, Paul's travel from Troas to Macedonia can be read as initiating a series of narratives wherein Paul is characterized as a Dionysian herald of Jesus, with rhetorical implications for those who oppose him.

The subsequent Philippian narrative, which continues through the end of the chapter (Acts 16:13-40), begins and ends with Paul's interactions with a woman appropriately named Lydia.[19] The narrative indicates that she was "a dealer of purple cloth, from the city of Thyatira, a worshipper of God" (16:14), and she listened to Paul and his companions "outside the gate" of Philippi, "near the river," which was apparently a place of prayer (16:13). Perhaps most striking here is Lydia's designation as being from Thyatira, a city in the region called Lydia within Asia Minor. Thus, both Lydia's name and her place of origin associate Luke's Paul with Dionysus in Euripides' *Bacchae*—Lydia from Thyatira in Lydia is receptive to Paul's preaching, just as Dionysus is supported by a group of Lydian bacchants. Other elements in the narrative reinforce this association. Purple is the color most associated with wine, and Dionysus is the god of—most prominently—wine. Paul meets Lydia at a place of prayer outside the gates of Philippi, and the worship of Dionysus and its associated ecstatic activity occur outside of Thebes. Finally, the narrative specifies—without obvious motivation—that

---

[19] See Shelly Matthews, *First Converts: Rich Pagan Women and the Rhetoric of Mission in Early Judaism and Christianity* (Contraversions: Jews and Other Differences; Stanford, CA: Stanford University Press, 2001), 72-95; MacDonald, "Classical Greek Poetry and the Acts of the Apostles," 465-67; and MacDonald, *Luke and Vergil*, 28-29.

Paul's encounter with Lydia takes place near a river, and Dionysus locates himself in relation to two rivers—Dirce and Ismenus—at the beginning of the *Bacchae* (*Bacch.* 5). Moreover, before they depart from Philippi, the narrative notes that Paul and his companions visit Lydia's household one final time (Acts 16:40).

Narrative elements that are equally evocative of Euripides' *Bacchae* appear later in the Philippian scene, when Paul is freed from prison by an earthquake but chooses not to escape.[20] Paul and Silas's imprisonment is precipitated by Paul's exorcism of a slave-girl possessed by a Pythian spirit (Acts 16:16–24).[21] Having lost access to their source of exploitative income, the slave-girl's owners accuse Paul and Silas before the city authorities of "promoting customs that are not lawful for us as Romans to accept or perform" (16:21). MacDonald observes, "This episode again resembles the *Bacchae*, where Pentheus, scandalized by the strange religious practices that he considered inappropriate for Greeks, arrested and imprisoned the god (215–262)."[22] In what follows, the resemblance of the Philippian narrative to the *Bacchae* only intensifies.

After a jailer places them in the innermost cell of a prison and "fastened their feet in the stocks" (Acts 16:24), Paul and Silas pass the time by praying and singing hymns (16:25). At midnight, an earthquake shakes the jail so violently that

---

[20] See MacDonald, "Classical Greek Poetry and the Acts of the Apostles," 482–86 and MacDonald, *Luke and Vergil*, 41–48. For a comparison of the prison break in Acts 4:24–31 with Euripides' *Bacchae*, see Ziegler, *Dionysos in der Apostelgeschichte*, 159–60 and MacDonald, *Luke and Vergil*, 42–43. For a comparison of the prison break in Acts 5:17–32 with the *Bacchae*, see Ziegler, *Dionysos in der Apostelgeschichte*, 160–62 and MacDonald, *Luke and Vergil*, 39–41.

[21] MacDonald reads this encounter as an imitation of Aeschylus, *Eum.* 24–34. See MacDonald, *Luke and Vergil*, 44–45.

[22] MacDonald, *Luke and Vergil*, 46.

"all of the doors were immediately opened and everyone's chains unfastened [πάντων τὰ δεσμὰ ἀνέθη]" (16:26). Toward the end of the second act of the *Bacchae*, Pentheus orders the guards to lock up the disguised Dionysus "near the horse stables so that he sees only pitch darkness" (*Bacch*. 509-10). In response, Dionysus threatens Pentheus, "But know well that as a punishment for these insults Dionysus will pursue you—the very god you claim doesn't exist. Since when you wrong us, it is him you throw into chains [ἐς δεσμοὺς]" (516-18). Act three of the *Bacchae* begins with an earthquake violently shaking Pentheus's palace in response to the Lydian bacchants' prayers for the liberation of the Dionysian priest (576-603). Clearly free, Dionysus emerges and explains to the chorus that, although Pentheus was under the impression that he had bound Dionysus's hands "in tight nooses," he had instead tied up a bull, as Dionysus watched with amusement (615-22).[23]

The Philippian narrative in Acts continues with the jailer's reaction. Upon waking and finding "the doors of the prison opened," the jailer "drew his dagger [μάχαιραν] and was about to kill himself, since he thought the prisoners had escaped" (Acts 16:27).[24] Just in time, however, Paul emerges

---

[23] See also *Bacch*. 443-50, where a soldier narrates to Pentheus how "the Theban Bacchae whom you shut up and seized and bound in chains at the public jail [δεσμοῖσι]" were liberated. He explains, "The chains [δεσμὰ], of their own accord [αὐτόματα], came loose from the women's feet and the keys unlocked the jailhouse doors without a human hand." Readers who recognize the verbal and thematic similarities of Luke's earlier prison-break narratives (Acts 5:17-32; 12:5-11) with *Bacch*. 443-50 would be likely to recognize the similarities that are also present in Acts 16 (especially the unfastening of the chains without human agency), even though the primary parallels here are with the apparent release of Dionysus from prison that occurs shortly thereafter.

[24] Barrett writes, "Presumably the gaoler would think that punishment for allowing the escape of the prisoners would be an alternative worse than suicide. Cf. 12.19. Again dramatic effect is

and assures the jailer that all of the prisoners are still present. The jailer, grateful for his life, engages Paul in a conversation about salvation. Paul instructs him, "Trust in the Lord Jesus, and you will be saved, you and your household" (16:31), and so the jailer and his household were baptized and rejoiced (16:32–34). In the *Bacchae*, after the earthquake set Pentheus into a panic, as Dionysus narrates, "Imagining that I had escaped, he . . . darted into the dark house with his dagger [ξίφος] drawn. Then Bromios [Dionysus] . . . made a light in the courtyard. Chasing eagerly after it, Pentheus rushed forward and tried to stab the shining [image], thinking he was slaying me" (*Bacch.* 627–31).[25] Exhausted, Pentheus eventually drops his dagger and lies down (635). Following the narration of these events to the Lydian bacchants, Pentheus arrives and engages Dionysus in contentious conversation. This dialogue culminates with Dionysus tricking Pentheus into spying on the activity of the Theban bacchants, a decision that results in the king's death and the punishment of Agave and Cadmus, his mother and grandfather.

The extensive and distinctive parallels that Acts 16 shares with the *Bacchae* function to characterize Paul as a Dionysian figure. He associates with a Lydian woman, he is liberated from bondage after an earthquake, and his would-be adversary draws his dagger but does not actually use it on his intended target. In contrast to the presentation of Dionysus in the *Bacchae* as an agent of death and exile, however, the Philippian narrative presents Paul as a herald of salvation.

---

heightened (and the question of v. 30 prepared for), but whether the detail is a probable one is questioned. *Begs.* 4.198 observes that . . . the earthquake would have been regarded by responsible authorities as a reasonable excuse" (*Acts of the Apostles*, 2:795).

[25] On the distinction between ξίφος (*Bacch.* 627) and μάχαιρα (Acts 16:27), see W. Michaelis, "μάχαιρα," *TDNT* 4:524–27, here 524: a μάχαιρα is "in Xenoph. Eq., 12, 11 a curved weapon as distinct from the ξίφος, the pointed weapon or sword."

Thus, for readers who are familiar with the characterization of Dionysus in Euripides' *Bacchae*, the Philippian narrative communicates that Paul was similar to Dionysus and that the early followers of Jesus were similar to the bacchants, with the qualification that the movement focused on Jesus offers salvation rather than vengeance—a transformative adaptation of a tragic literary model. Furthermore, by evoking the storyline of the *Bacchae* and casting Paul as Dionysus, the narrative of Acts encourages readers to associate those who oppose Paul with the god-fighting Pentheus.

Reading Acts 17 with Euripides' Bacchae

What transpires in Thessalonica and Beroea (Acts 17:1-15) should thus be read within the context of these preceding narratives, especially their evocation of the plot of Euripides' *Bacchae* and their association of Paul with Dionysus. Such contextualization prepares readers to observe that the Thessalonian narrative continues this allusive trend. Most notable in this regard are the narrative's inclusion of prominent women among those convinced by Paul and the anxiety-driven opposition to Paul's proclamation, which quickly escalates to involve the city authorities.

The Thessalonian narrative in Acts indicates that "not a few leading women" (Acts 17:4) were among those persuaded by the proclamation of Paul and Silas in the synagogue. To be sure, this is neither the first nor the last time that the Acts narrative includes a notice about women receiving the message proclaimed by followers of Jesus favorably.[26] What *is* noteworthy is the narrative's generalization of them as "leading [πρώτων]" women. On two other occasions, including the subsequent Beroean episode (Acts 17:12), the

---

[26] E.g., Acts 5:14; 8:12; 13:50; 17:12. Moreover, Saul—imitating Pentheus—rages against the church, persecuting "both men and women" (Acts 8:3; 9:2; 22:4).

narrative similarly characterizes women who respond favorably to Paul's preaching as "prominent [εὐσχημόνων]."[27] Several twentieth-century commentators have argued, however, that their inclusion in Acts 17:4—and presumably also in 17:12—makes little sense within the narrative. For example, Joseph A. Fitzmyer reports, "Both Haenchen (*Acts*, 507) and Conzelmann (*Acts*, 135) find it strange that such prominent women would not have been able to avert the persecutions of Christians."[28] To these commentators, the references to prominent women thus appear to be non sequiturs. Nevertheless, their inclusion does follow when considered in the context of the narrative's evident use of the *Bacchae* as a literary model. Just as elite women are prominent among the followers of Dionysus in Thebes, so the Thessalonian and Beroean narratives foreground the positive responses of elite women to Paul's preaching. Doing so reinforces the association of Paul with Dionysus.

Following Paul's favorable reception among elite women in Thessalonica and Beroea, the Acts narratives describe opposition to Paul. The Thessalonian narrative explains only that "the Jews became jealous, and, taking some bad men from the marketplace and starting a riot, they set the city in an uproar" (Acts 17:5). Failing to locate Paul and Silas, they drag Jason and some of his comrades before the city authorities, accusing them of sedition (17:6–7). The Beroean narrative similarly notes that "when the Jews of Thessalonica learned that the word of God had been preached by Paul also in Beroea, they came there too, agitating and stirring up the

---

[27] The other is Acts 13:50. See also Matthews, *First Converts*, 51–71.

[28] Joseph A. Fitzmyer, *The Acts of the Apostles: A New Translation with Introduction and Commentary* (AB 31; New York: Doubleday, 1998), 595. See Ernst Haenchen, *The Acts of the Apostles: A Commentary* (Oxford: Blackwell, 1971), 507 and Hans Conzelmann, *Acts of the Apostles: A Commentary on the Acts of the Apostles* (Hermeneia; Philadelphia: Fortress, 1987), 135.

crowds" (17:13). In the *Bacchae*, Pentheus's opposition to Dionysus is motivated by his anxiety concerning the participation of prominent Theban women—including his mother and aunts—in a reputedly licentious religious cult. Pentheus thus imprisons the Lydian bacchants and even the disguised Dionysus himself, albeit only temporarily in both cases.

The Thessalonian and Beroean narratives in Acts thus exhibit a pattern that broadly reflects the plot of Euripides' *Bacchae*, as the following table demonstrates.

Euripides' *Bacchae*	Acts 17:1-9	Acts 17:10-15
Dionysus and a maenad cohort arrive in Thebes from Lydia (*Bacch.* 1, 55-56)	[Paul and company previously sailed from Troas to Macedonia (Acts 16:11-12)]	[Paul and company previously sailed from Troas to Macedonia (Acts 16:11-12)]
	Paul and Silas arrive in Thessalonica (17:1)	Paul and Silas arrive in Beroea (17:10)
Dionysus's religious movement is popular among Theban women (see, e.g., 215-25, 677-774)	Paul preaches in the synagogue, and "many devout Greeks and not a few leading women" are convinced (17:4)	Paul preaches in the synagogue and "not a few prominent Greek women and men" believed (17:12)
Rumors of sexual impropriety (see, e.g., 215-25)	—	—

Euripides' *Bacchae*	Acts 17:1–9	Acts 17:10–15
Pentheus, king of Thebes, expresses anxiety on account of the Bacchic movement (see, e.g., 215–25, 453–60)	Some Thessalonian Jews "become jealous" (17:5a)	"But when the Jews from Thessalonica learned that the word of God had been proclaimed by Paul also in Beroea . . ." (17:13a)
Pentheus opposes the priest of the Dionysian cult (see, e.g., 233–47, 352–57)	These Thessalonian Jews oppose Paul, fomenting a riot and enlisting the aid of city authorities (Acts 17:5–6)	". . . they came [to Beroea] too, agitating and stirring up the crowds" (Acts 17:13b)

Interpretability: The Scandal of Gentile Inclusion

What remains to be explored is the substance of what the Acts narrative communicates about Paul and the early followers of Jesus by modeling their presentation on the plot of Euripides' *Bacchae*. As the table above highlights, the Thessalonian and Beroean narratives both lack intimations of sexual scandal, and this deviation from the Euripidean pattern may be instructive with respect to the narrative's vision of the kingdom of God and its characterization of those who reject Jesus and his followers. Although rumors of sexual impropriety triggered Pentheus's anxiety, precipitating his opposition to the Dionysian cult, readers of Acts are unable to so easily connect the positive response of the elite women, on the one hand, to the opposition of certain Jews, on the other. Nevertheless, it may be possible for readers to make sense of the narrative pattern exhibited in Thessalonica and Beroea by accounting for both of the identity markers specified among those who are receptive to Paul's message. Accordingly, readers might regard the specification of the *female* identity of some of those who believed Paul as a narrative element designed to associate Paul with Dionysus, while interpreting the *other* specified identity as explaining the anxiety of the unconvinced Jews: namely, some of those who receive Paul's message favorably are identified as "Greeks," or Gentiles.[29]

Thus, in addition to including "not a few leading women" among those convinced by Paul in Thessalonica, the narrative also mentions "a great many God-fearing Greeks [τῶν . . . σεβομένων Ἑλλήνων πλῆθος πολύ]" (17:4). Similarly, in Beroea, Paul convinces "not a few prominent Greek women and men" (17:12) — foregrounding their non-Judean ethnicity alongside their gender and social status. The inclusion of Greek God-fearers with the elite women — alongside the absence of sexual scandal — can alert readers to a mimetic reconfiguration: the substitution of Gentile inclusion for rumors of sexual impropriety. By presenting a story about Gentile inclusion in this way, the narrative of Acts communicates at least two ideas.

First, the substitution of Gentile inclusion for sexual scandal in Acts 17 suggests that the inclusion of Gentiles ought to be regarded as a prominent feature of the Jesus movement. Whether to include Gentiles among God's people — and, if so, to what extent and under what conditions — was an active debate among Jews in the Second Temple period and beyond. Indeed, the narrative of Acts dramatizes this debate in chapter 15 with the Council of Jerusalem as well as in the earlier account of Peter and

---

[29] This interpretation of the motivation of Paul's Thessalonian opponents coheres with other narratives in Acts. Most notably, Saul/Paul is opposed by a Judean false prophet in Cyprus (Acts 13:4–12). Specifically, the false prophet seeks "to turn the proconsul [Sergius Paulus, a Gentile] from the faith" (13:8), exhibiting a comparable anxiety about the inclusion of a Gentile in the kingdom of God.

Cornelius.[30] The Thessalonian and Beroean narratives in Acts 17 can thus be read as expressing the narrative's position emphatically: Gentiles can indeed be integrated into the people of God. In fact, not only is this the position of the Jesus movement, those with the appropriate cultural competence can further interpret the Acts 17 narratives as suggesting that Gentile inclusion is as characteristic of the Jesus movement as reputations for sexual impropriety are of Dionysian religion, not least as it is portrayed in Euripides' *Bacchae*.

Second, much like the use of the Biblical prophet framework in Luke 4, the substitution in Acts 17 eases readers' concerns about the rejection of the followers of Jesus by certain Jews. Rather than associating Paul with Biblical Hebrew prophets, however, it does so by correlating the rejection of Paul and his preaching to Gentiles with Pentheus's opposition to Dionysus's cult. Both frameworks—Israelite rejection of prophets and Pentheus's opposition to Dionysus—constitute culturally meaningful ways to communicate that rejection from a certain group need not undermine the credibility of a particular figure or movement. Moreover, the association of Paul's opponents with Pentheus can have the rhetorical effect of projecting the readers' negative evaluations of Pentheus onto Paul's Thessalonian opponents. This projection may particularly affect readers' judgments regarding Gentile inclusion, since it appears to be the salient feature motivating their opposition to Paul's preaching.

---

[30] For the account of Peter and Cornelius, see Michael Kochenash, "Reconsidering Luke-Acts and Virgil's *Aeneid*: Negotiating Ethnic Legacies," *Christian Origins and the New Testament in the Greco-Roman Context: Essays in Honor of Dennis R. MacDonald* (ed. Margaret Froelich et al.; CSNTCO 1; Claremont, CA: Claremont Press, 2016), 7–38, here 28–37, and Michael Kochenash, "Cornelius's Obeisance to Peter (Acts 10:25–26) and Judaea Capta Coins," *CBQ*, forthcoming.

Conclusion

The narrative of Acts thus characterizes Paul as a Dionysian herald of a religious movement, associates those who oppose Paul with the god-fighter Pentheus, and emphasizes the status of Gentile inclusion as a central feature of the Jesus movement. In doing so, Acts 17:1-15 blends together the reasonings associated with the plot of Euripides' *Bacchae* and the Jason myth. Those who accuse the Christians of sedition are motivated to do so on account of their anxiety about elite women and Gentiles responding positively to Paul's preaching. Although the narrative reasoning associated with the name Jason appears to support the contention of Paul's opponents regarding a threat to the political order, their credibility is undermined by the narrator. Their opposition is further discredited by being associated with Pentheus's persecution of Dionysus and the bacchants.

As with Jesus in Luke 4, the narrative of Acts presents the rejection of Paul and his preaching within the framework of a familiar antecedent narrative. By reading Acts 17:1-15 with Euripides' *Bacchae*, readers can observe a Euripidean pattern in the Thessalonian and Beroean narratives. Notably absent from Acts 17:1-15, however, is any indication of sexual impropriety. In its place within the narrative pattern, however, readers can find the inclusion of Gentiles. Readers of Acts can thus associate opponents of Gentile inclusion with Pentheus's rash opposition to Dionysus, and they can interpret these Acts narratives as suggesting that Gentile inclusion is as characteristic of the Jesus movement as sexual scandal is of Dionysus's movement. Thus, according to certain narratives in Luke and Acts, Jewish opponents of the Lukan kingdom of God are like the Israelites who rejected the true prophets, and they are also like Pentheus—god-fighters.

Objections, Reflections, and Anticipations
Dennis R. MacDonald

I am profoundly grateful to the contributors to this volume, especially to Mark G. Bilby, who have devoted their erudition to *The Gospels and Homer, Luke and Vergil,* and *The Dionysian Gospel*.[1] Even though I take exception to several criticisms, my responses in no way diminish that heartfelt gratitude. My brief responses obviously do not permit the exhaustive attention that these contributions deserve, but I trust that my comments will suffice to advance the discussion.

Defending Mimesis Criticism

Although most essays express misgivings about details of my comparisons of New Testament narratives to classical Greek literature, none so broadly dismisses them as Kay Higuera Smith in "Mark and Homer." She concedes many of the parallels but argues, as have others, for an "indirect" influence rather than a strategic and hermeneutically freighted direct one.

Neither the Markan author's socioeconomic nor sociolinguistic location make it likely that Mark could have had the education or the rhetorical training that would be required to argue with sufficient plausibility that he followed

---

[1] Dennis R. MacDonald, *The Gospels and Homer: Imitations of Greek Epic in Mark and Luke-Acts* (NTGL 1; Lanham, MD: Rowman & Littlefield, 2015); Dennis R. MacDonald, *Luke and Vergil: Imitations of Classical Greek Literature* (NTGL 2; Lanham, MD: Rowman & Littlefield, 2015); and Dennis R. MacDonald, *The Dionysian Gospel: The Fourth Gospel and Euripides* (Minneapolis: Fortress, 2017).

ancient models of Greek education by consistently and directly imitating Homer and other classical Greek sources.[2]

To support this objection Smith asserts that "Mark's marginal socioeconomic status and his poor grammatical skills would have made a classical education unlikely."[3] She obviously knows much more about the anonymous author's "socioeconomic status" than I. Concern for "those of low social status" by no means was restricted to the marginal themselves, as the Lukan Evangelist amply illustrates. Such concerns appear also in the Homeric epics and Athenian tragedies and among many other texts by cultural elites. I strongly disagree that distaste for taxation, slavery, and "economic exploitation" were "not the concerns of social elites but of those who identify with the social margins."[4]

On the other hand, Smith rightly complains that Mark's syntax leaves much to be desired and that his vocabulary is pedestrian; even so, his skills as a narrator are extraordinary. This apparent contradiction, however, appears in other works known for their imitations of classical Greek poetry, such as the Book of Judith—which similarly displays significant Semitic interference—3 Maccabees, and the Testament of Abraham. Among Christian texts I would adduce the Acts of Andrew and the City of the Cannibals and the Passion and Resurrection of Jesus Written by Aeneas the Jew, a Byzantine recension of the Gospel of Nicodemus. The best-known pagan imitations of Homer appear in Vergil and Lucian, but many others appear in compositions by *hoi polloi*. Some authors even complained about how common they were.

I do, however, concede that that some of the parallels between Mark and Homer might be indirect, as the

---

[2] Kay Higuera Smith, "Mark and Homer," *supra*.
[3] Smith, "Mark and Homer," *supra*.
[4] Smith, "Mark and Homer," *supra*.

contribution by Richard C. Miller illustrates.[5] I suspect that Luke's story of Jesus's ascension imitates Livy's Latin account of the ascension of Romulus, whereas Miller prefers a less direct, broadly cultural influence of mythologies of postmortem exaltations of kings and emperors.[6]

But even if some parallels are not direct, others surely are. Perhaps I could have distinguished, as I have elsewhere, between the author's occasional direct and visual imitating and the readers' memory or non-textual exposure to Homeric episodes and characters. Clearly the Markan Evangelist could not have expected his readers to have had access to these scrolls. I created the seven criteria of Mimesis Criticism in large measure to establish whether parallels between any two texts imply a direct or indirect imitation—or no mimesis at all. I am, however, gratified by Smith's gracious conclusion that "no study of the New Testament henceforth can ignore the classical literature of ancient Greece."[7]

Refining Mimesis Criticism

I know of no more penetrating and provocative assessment of the avoidance of Mimesis Criticism in the history of New Testament scholarship and higher education than the opening section of Mark Bilby's "Mainstreaming Mimesis Criticism." Exposure to classical Greek literature—especially Homeric epic and Athenian tragedy, the intellectual foundations of Greek identity in the early Roman Empire—is almost entirely absent in departments of religion and theological seminaries. Miller similarly speaks of "an

---

[5] Richard C. Miller, "Neos Dionysos in Textual and Cultural Mimesis," *supra*.
[6] See MacDonald, *Luke and Vergil*, 196–200.
[7] Smith, "Mark and Homer," *supra*.

altogether sad, pandemic-level lack of training and familiarity with classical culture in the Romano-Greek East."[8]

The trilogy of my books attempts to compensate for this cultural void, but Bilby rightly notes that

> One person may pioneer a movement, but he cannot make it. As mimesis criticism becomes more mainstream and widespread, it must become more nuanced, more diverse, and yes, more provisional and more contentious, too. MacDonald's pioneering effort … is invaluable. Yet, as primarily the work of one person rather than a community or school, it is inevitably going to be idiosyncratic at points.[9]

Later he adds: "Mimesis Criticism must move beyond one person and become a shared methodology and discourse."[10] As I understand it, this was the driving force behind the collection of essays that comprise this volume. The idiosyncrasies of my work include, says Bilby, advocating for direct literary parallels that are less compelling than others or that one might explain otherwise, such as rhetorical topoi, or popular culture, or the influence of the Septuagint, which I have never denied. In many cases, one finds multiple antetextual influences and intertextual strategies, such as quotation, allusion, and redaction.

Several contributions to this volume clarify the various literary and theological motivations for mimesis of classical Greek texts, a topic highlighted by Michael Kochenash in "Even Good Homer Nods," and more urgently advocated by Chan Sok Park, who presses for more attention to "the politics of imitation."[11] For example, Park asks if Dionysian influence

---

[8] Miller, "Neos Dionysos," *supra*.

[9] Mark G. Bilby, "Mainstreaming Mimesis Criticism," *supra*.

[10] Bilby, "Mainstreaming Mimesis Criticism," *supra*.

[11] Michael Kochenash, "Even Good Homer Nods," *supra* and Chan Sok Park, "John's Politics of Imitation," *supra*.

on the Fourth Gospel reflects the origins of the Johannine tradition and not merely the literary creativity of the author. Furthermore, he asks if attention to mimesis of Euripides and the complex compositional history of the Gospel might shed light on the development of "the Johannine community."

Because of such intramural disputes among mimesis critics, Bilby advocates extensive and collaborative evaluations of such proposals among scholars in professional meetings in order to rank their plausibility and significance.[12] Such collaborations would address Miller's observation that scholars too frequently dismiss a new hypothesis "by pointing out its weakest link."[13] One might say that the volume at hand is an initial step in the direction of identifying the most compelling mimetic connections.

In his response to *The Dionysian Gospel*, Bilby provides another example of differences among practitioners of Mimesis Criticism; namely, how best to integrate this new methodology with alternatives.[14] For example, he finds compelling recent work on Luke-Acts that dates the final redaction as late as 150 CE, late enough to argue against an early form of Marcionism as expressed in a hypothetical reconstruction of a putative primitive version of Luke, without Acts. According to Bilby, "the first edition of John," the Dionysian Gospel, "used Luke, but not the final version" of it but the anti-Marcionite final redaction.[15] He thus argues that the direction of dependence at this stage moves in the other direction, from John to Luke.

He bolsters this conclusion with two observations: first, many Lukan pericopae find no equivalents in John. I would

---

[12] Bilby, "Mainstreaming Mimesis Criticism," *supra*.

[13] Miller, "Neos Dionysos," *supra*.

[14] Mark G. Bilby, "The First Dionysian Gospel: Imitational and Redactional Layers in Luke and John," *supra*.

[15] Bilby, "The First Dionysian Gospel," *supra*.

counter that authors have no obligation to use anything in their sources. Second, Bilby finds support for this view in Pliny's correspondence with Trajan on the Christian movement in Asia Minor, which he sees as a historical watershed for both Luke and John; in each case, an earlier version of the Gospel precedes it and one or more later versions follow it.

I have no principled problem with the notion that Marcion knew a Gospel different from and shorter than the text known to the likes of Irenaeus, Tertullian, Epiphanius, and others, but I do find exceedingly problematic the view that the proposed pre-Marcion Luke was Ur-Lukas, the Evangelist's original composition. All of the competing reconstructions of the pre-Marcion Gospel share the following characteristics: like the canonical Lukan Gospel, the hypothetical earlier truncated version follows the Markan sequence and carefully redacts it. However one views Luke's agreements with Matthew against Mark—either as evidence of Q/Q+ or Matthew—the two proposed compositional strata share the same redactional tendencies. And what is most relevant to the book at hand, both compositional strata display the same mimetic creativity on the same models, Homer and the Bacchae, though they are greatly expanded in Acts. I fear that the hoopla over the recovery of a likely pre-Marcion *Evangelikon* will blind future researchers to the literary and brilliant consistency throughout the Gospel as we now have it.

My conclusion to this volume obviously is not the place to criticize Bilby's creative proposal in detail; rather, it is the place to thank him for providing an example of methodological eclecticism that takes Mimesis Criticism seriously. Mimesis is a new and promising tool, but it is not the only one in the exegetical shed. Gospel texts are notoriously complex and thus require multiple methodological approaches. Mimesis is messy and, despite my application of criteria to diminish the subjectivity of identifying it, the venture remains vexing. Scholars inevitably disagree. I warmly welcome Bilby's proposal that what now is too often my idiolect become a scholarly sociolect. I am far less interested in making faithful disciples than in making waves that one day will wash ashore even at the beaches of contemporary religion, which brings me to Bilby's other major concern.

"For mimesis to get a fair hearing, we also must address faith-based approaches to the New Testament and how Mimesis Criticism relates to them."[16] I make no apologies that I am a Christian who evaluates religious language, including God-talk, as a cultural anthropologist and not as a believer. I am a humanist who studies religion as someone colorblind might study Renaissance oil painting. In many cases, one does not need historical bedrock or even antecedent tradition to explain New Testament narratives or the existence of many characters, but there are exceptions, and Bilby rightly notes that I do not deny the existence of Paul even though the Acts of the Apostles portrays him as a Christian Socrates.[17] Kochenash notes that Mark seems to have burnished traditions about John the Baptist by imitating the beheading of Agamemnon in Greek epic and tragedy.[18]

I make a similar claim for Jesus himself in *Mythologizing Jesus: From Jewish Teacher to Epic Hero*.[19] I am not a mythicist: of course Jesus existed, but he also soon became the target of mythologizing to compete with Jewish and Greek gods and heroes. On the other hand, I am highly skeptical that the following Gospel characters ever existed: Mary Magdalene, Judas Iscariot, Joseph of Arimathea, the young man who fled

---

[16] Bilby, "Mainstreaming Mimesis Criticism," *supra*.

[17] Bilby, "Mainstreaming Mimesis Criticism," *supra*. See also Ilseo Park, "Acts 2 as an Intertextual Map: Moving from Dionysian to Platonic Identity," *supra*.

[18] Kochenash, "Even Good Homer Nods," *supra*.

[19] Dennis R. MacDonald, *Mythologizing Jesus: From Jewish Teacher to Epic Hero* (Lanham, MD: Rowman & Littlefield, 2015).

at Jesus's arrest, and many others.[20] Similarly, the existence of the following characters in the Acts of the Apostles is highly problematic: the Ethiopian eunuch, Aeneas, Dorcas, Cornelius, Eutychus, Jason, and others.[21] Obviously, such skepticism is not shared by the vast majority of Christian believers, including many New Testament critics.

Literary assessments may inform but need not be determinative for making historical judgments, as the examples of the Baptist and Jesus in Mark and Paul in Acts demonstrate. It is one thing to argue, as I do, that one does not need historical events or characters to explain their appearance in early Christian narratives, but it is quite another dogmatically to deny their existence. Kochenash makes a similar suggestion which merits repeating:

> some readers will likely be turned off by MacDonald's assertion that Mark and Luke created narratives from scratch in order to imitate literary models. Instead, an agnostic approach might be more palatable for a broader reading public. Mark and Luke may have created narratives inspired by nothing more than their

---

[20] For Mary Magdalene, see MacDonald, *Gospels and Homer*, 13 and 94–98. For Judas Iscariot, see MacDonald, *Gospels and Homer*, 11–12, 281–82, and 315–18. For Joseph of Arimathea, see MacDonald, *Gospels and Homer*, 104–12. For the young man at Jesus's arrest, see MacDonald, *Gospels and Homer*, 247–50.

[21] For the Ethiopian eunuch, see MacDonald, *Gospels and Homer*, 113–17. For Aeneas, see MacDonald, *Gospels and Homer*, 47–49; see also Michael Kochenash, "You Can't Hear 'Aeneas' without Thinking of Rome," *JBL* 136.3 (2017): 667–85. For Dorcas, see MacDonald, *Gospels and Homer*, 138–40; see also Michael Kochenash, "Political Correction: Luke's Tabitha (Acts 9:36-43), Virgil's Dido, and Cleopatra," *NovT* 60.1 (2018): 1–13. For Cornelius, see Dennis R. MacDonald, *Does the New Testament Imitate Homer? Four Cases from the Acts of the Apostles* (New Haven: Yale University Press, 2003), 2–65 and MacDonald, *Gospels and Homer*, 33–46. For Eutychus, see Dennis R. MacDonald, "Luke's Eutychus and Homer's Elpenor: Acts 20:7-12 and *Odyssey* 10–12," *JHC* 1.1 (1994): 5–24 and MacDonald, *Gospels and Homer*, 226–29. For Jason, see MacDonald, *Luke and Vergil*, 48–50.

literary models on occasion. At other times, however, they may have been inspired to elaborate their compositions due to the similarities between traditions about Jesus, Peter, and Paul and certain exemplary literary models.[22]

Later he adds: "I wonder whether an agnosticism about possible sources [e.g., reliable oral tradition] could have improved the chances of positive reception among moderate conservatives on the one hand and liberals approaching the narratives from a twentieth-century form-critical framework on the other."[23]

But Bilby goes much further in making a case for the value of Mimesis Criticism for Christian believers:

> Time and again, what struck me in MacDonald's works were the ways in which mimesis critical readings underscored a *high* Christology. The Jesuses of Mark, Luke, and John not only surpassingly emulate the roles and feats of epic heroes, but even those of epic deities. One might see in many mimesis critical readings so many opportunities for theologians and preachers to proclaim a Christ that does not merely recall but indeed completely surpasses all other models and objects of devotion.[24]

He goes on to suggest that the influence of Greek literature on the high Christologies of the Gospels historically established the terms of debate for later theological disputes. Put otherwise, Mimesis Criticism does not trivialize the Jesus of the Gospels but exalts him.

Indeed, the Christological controversies of ancient Christianity can easily be read as the profoundly

---

[22] Kochenash, "Even Good Homer Nods," *supra*.
[23] Kochenash, "Even Good Homer Nods," *supra*.
[24] Bilby, "Introduction: Mainstreaming Mimesis Criticism," *supra*.

difficult effort to come to terms with the implications of the appropriation of classical models in the Gospels. How to reconcile Jewish monotheism with the epic depictions of Jesus—this lies at the heart of early Christian theological debates and liturgies. These debates also repeatedly evince a lively tension between competing appropriations of Greek epic and Greek philosophy. As readers will see later, this tension stood at the core of the emergence of proto-Orthodox/Catholic Christianity and was already very much in evidence in Acts and the later redactional layers of the Gospel of John and Gospel of Luke. Even outside of Christian circles, we find that the primary objections lodged by rabbinic Judaism and Islam against Jesus's deification and Trinitarian theology demonstrate an incisive awareness of the patently obvious connections between classical stories and early Christian claims, and an informed objection to Christian theology being a legitimate appropriation of Jewish monotheism and Greek philosophy.[25]

According to Bilby, the tracing of Greek poetic influence on such disputes thus is "a massive area for future research."[26] It also helps in understanding the high Christologies in much of modern Christendom.

Expanding Mimesis Criticism

The last three contributions in this volume offer further explorations of my applications of Mimesis Criticism. Austin Busch shows that Mark's story of the Gerasene demoniac, a likely imitation of Homer's Polyphemus, finds a later analogy in Philostratus's clever use of Polyphemus in the *Life of*

---

[25] Bilby, "Mainstreaming Mimesis Criticism," *supra*.
[26] Bilby, "Mainstreaming Mimesis Criticism," *supra*.

Apollonius.[27] Even more significant, in my view, are his references to analogous imitations of the Homeric tale in texts earlier than Philostratus, such as Theocritus's *Idylls* 6 and 11 and especially Vergil's *Aeneid* book 3.

Ilseo Park insightfully explores how the author of the Acts of the Apostles shifted the Dionysian madness of Pentecost into the Platonic political idealism of pooled wealth in Acts 2 (and 4).[28] Furthermore, he notes that in *Luke and Vergil* I argued that the parallels with the *Bacchae* appear predominantly in Acts 1-16 and those with Plato and Xenophon predominantly in Acts 17-28 where Luke portrays Paul as a Christianized Socrates. Park's original contribution is to propose that Acts 2 prepares the reader to see in the narrative a transition from Dionysian enthusiasm to Socratic philosophical sophistication. Kochenash similarly points out this transition from parallels between the Euripidean Dionysus and Paul in Thessalonica in Acts 17:1–15, on the one hand, and between the Platonic Socrates and Paul in Athens in 17:16–34, on the other.[29]

I warmly welcome these insightful expansions of my work and encourage the application of Mimesis Criticism not only to the canonical Gospels and Acts but also to extracanonical Jewish and Christian literature, without ignoring the importance of the methodology to fictional composition in antiquity more generally. Among my own forthcoming publications I will mention *Luke and the Politics of Homeric Imitation: Luke-Acts as a Rival to the* Aeneid and "The Jewish Agave and Hera: A Mimetic Reading the Book of Judith," which argues for imitations of the *Bacchae* and *Il.* 14.

---

[27] Austin Busch, "Scriptural Revision in Mark's Gospel and Philostratus's *Life of Apollonius*," *supra.*

[28] Park, "Acts 2 as an Intertextual Map," *supra.*

[29] Michael Kochenash, "The Scandal of Gentile Inclusion: Reading Acts 17 with Euripides' *Bacchae*," *supra.*

In the first half of *From the Earliest Gospel (Q+) and the Gospel of Mark: Solving the Synoptic Problem with Mimesis Criticism*, I will argue that the lost Gospel extensively and polemically imitated the Book of Deuteronomy to portray Jesus as the promised prophet like Moses. In the second half, I use Mimesis Criticism to examine the vexing overlaps between Q/Q+ in the Gospel of Mark. In other words, this underutilized methodology sheds light on the echoes of Jewish scriptures in the lost Gospel and on Mark's eclectic imitations not only of the Homeric epics but also the earliest Gospel. It is my hope that these studies, together with the work of scholars such as the contributors to this volume, will propel this methodology toward the center of New Testament scholarship, as Mark Bilby has advocated.

Bibliography

Adams, Sean A. "Luke and *Progymnasmata*: Rhetorical Handbooks, Rhetorical Sophistication and Genre Selection." *Ancient Education and Early Christianity*, 137–54. Edited by Matthew Ryan Hauge and Andrew W. Pitts. LNTS 533. London: Bloomsbury T&T Clark, 2016.

Allen, Thomas W., ed. *Homeri Opera*. 2nd ed. OCT. Oxford: Clarendon, 1917.

Anderson, Graham. *The Second Sophistic: A Cultural Phenomenon in the Roman Empire*. London: Routledge, 1993.

Apollonius Rhodius. *Argonautica*. Edited and translated by William H. Race. LCL. Cambridge, MA: Harvard University Press, 2009.

Attridge, Harold W. "Genre." *How John Works: Storytelling in the Fourth Gospel*, 7–22. Edited by Douglas Estes and Ruth Sheridan. Atlanta: SBL, 2016.

Attridge, Harold W. "Paul and Pentheus: What's in a Possible Allusion." *Delightful Acts: New Essays on Canonical and Non-Canonical Acts*, 7–18. Edited by Harold W. Attridge, Dennis R. MacDonald, and Clare K. Rothschild. WUNT I/391. Tübingen: Mohr Siebeck, 2017.

Aulén, Gustaf. *Christus Victor: An Historical Study of the Three Main Types of the Idea of the Atonement*. Translated by A. G. Herbert. New York: Macmillan, 1969.

Barrett, C. K. *A Critical and Exegetical Commentary on the Acts of the Apostles*. 2 vols. ICC 34. Edinburgh: T&T Clark, 1994–1998.

Baur, Ferdinand Christian. "Apollonius von Tyana und Christus oder das Verhältniss des Pythagoreismus zum Christentum. Ein Beitrag zur Religionsgeschichte der ersten Jarhunderte nach Christus." *Drei Abhandlungen zur Geschichte der alten Philosophie und ihres Verhältnisses zum Christentum*, 1–227. Edited by Eduard Zeller. Leipzig: Fues's Verlag, 1876.

Becker, Eve-Marie, Troels Engberg-Pedersen, and Mogens Müller, eds. *Mark and Paul: Comparative Essays Part II: For and Against Pauline Influence on Mark*. BZNW 199. Berlin: de Gruyter, 2014.

BeDuhn, Jason D. "The Myth of Marcion as Redactor: The Evidence of Marcion's Gospel against an Assumed Marcionite Redaction." *Annali di storia dell'esegesi* 29.1 (2012): 21–48.

Belo, Fernando. *A Materialist Reading of the Gospel of Mark*. Maryknoll, NY: Orbis, 1975.

Blumenthal, Christian. *Basileia bei Lukas: Studien zur erzählerischen Entfaltung der lukanischen Basileiakonzeption*. HBS 84. Freiburg: Herder, 2016.

Bilby, Mark G. "Pliny's Correspondence and the Acts of the Apostles: An Intertextual Relationship." *Luke on Jesus, Paul and Christianity: What Did He Really Know?*, 147–69. Edited by Joseph Verheyden and John S. Kloppenborg. BTS 29. Leuven: Peeters, 2017.

Bonner, Campbell. "The Technique of Exorcism." *HTR* 36.1 (1943): 39–49.

Boter, Gerard. "Towards a New Critical Edition of Philostratus' *Life of Apollonius*: The Affiliation of the Manuscripts." *Theios Sophistes: Essays on Flavius Philostratus'* Vita Apollonii, 21–56. Edited by Kristoffel Demoen and Danny Praet. Leiden: Brill, 2009.

Brant, Jo-Ann A. *Dialogue and Drama: Elements of Greek Tragedy in the Fourth Gospel*. Peabody, MA: Hendrickson, 2004.

Brodie, Thomas L. "The Accusing and Stoning of Naboth (1 Kgs 21:8–13) as One Component of the Stephen Text (Acts 6:9–14; 7:58a)." *CBQ* 45.3 (1983): 417–32.

Brodie, Thomas L. "Greco-Roman Imitation of Texts as a Partial Guide to Luke's Use of Sources." *Luke-Acts: New*

Brodie, Thomas L. *Perspectives from the Society of Biblical Literature Seminar*, 17–46. Edited by Charles H. Talbert. New York: Crossroad, 1984.

Brodie, Thomas L. "Luke-Acts as an Imitation and Emulation of the Elijah-Elisha Narrative." *New Views on Luke and Acts*, 78–85. Edited by Earl Richard. Wilmington: Glazier, 1983.

Brodie, Thomas L. "Not Q but Elijah: The Saving of the Centurion's Slave (Luke 7:1–10) as an Internalization of the Saving of the Widow and Her Child." *IBS* 14.2 (1992): 54–71.

Brodie, Thomas L. "Towards Unraveling Luke's Use of the Old Testament: Luke 7.11–17 as an *Imitatio* of 1 Kings 17.17–24." *NTS* 32.2 (1986): 247–67.

Brookins, Timothy A. "Luke's Use of Mark as παράφρασις: Its Effects on Characterization in the 'Healing of Blind Bartimeaus' Pericope (Mark 10.46–52/Luke 18.35–43)." *JSNT* 34.1 (2011): 70–89.

Bruce, F. F. *The Book of the Acts*. Rev. ed. NICNT. Grand Rapids: Eerdmans, 1988.

Bultmann, Rudolf. *The Theology of the New Testament*. Translated by Kendrick Grobel. 2 vols. New York: Scribners, 1951–1955.

Busch, Austin "Characterizing Gnostic Scriptural Interpretation." *ZAC* 21.2 (2017): 243–72.

Busch, Austin "Gnostic Biblical and Second Sophistic Homeric Interpretation." *ZAC*, forthcoming.

Busch, Austin 22.2 (2018): 195-217 "Gnostic Exegesis of Genesis and Second-Sophistic Readings of Homer: Prolegomenon to the Study of Post-Classical Revisionary Scriptural Interpretation." *ZAC*, forthcoming.

Carhart, Ryan. "The Second Sophistic and the Cultural Idealization of Paul in Acts." *Engaging Early Christian History: Reading Acts in the Second Century*, 187–208.

Edited by Rubén R. Dupertuis and Todd Penner. London: Routledge, 2014.

Carter, Warren. "Cross-Gendered Romans and Mark's Jesus: Legion Enters the Pigs (Mark 5:1–20)." *JBL* 134.1 (2015): 139–55.

Collins, Adela Yarbro. *Mark: A Commentary*. Edited by Harold W. Attridge. Hermeneia. Minneapolis: Fortress, 2007.

Conzelmann, Hans. *Acts of the Apostles: A Commentary on the Acts of the Apostles*. Hermeneia. Philadelphia: Fortress, 1987.

Crossan, John Dominic. "Empty Tomb and Absent Lord (Mark 16:1–8)." *The Passion in Mark: Studies on Mark 14–16*, 135–52. Edited by Werner H. Kelber. Philadelphia: Fortress, 1976.

D'Angelo, Mary Rose. "The ANHP Question in Luke-Acts: Imperial Masculinity and the Deployment of Women in the Early Second Century." *A Feminist Companion to Luke*, 44–69. Edited by Amy-Jill Levine. Feminist Companion to the New Testament and Early Christian Writings 3. Sheffield: Sheffield Academic Press, 2002.

Danker, Frederick W. "The Demonic Secret in Mark: A Reexamination of the Cry of Dereliction (15.34)." *ZNW* 61.1–2 (1970): 48–69.

Dijk, Gert-Jan van. "The *Odyssey* of Apollonius: An Intertextual Paradigm." *Philostratus*, 176–202. Edited by Ewen Bowie and Jaś Elsner. Greek Culture in the Roman World. Cambridge: Cambridge University Press, 2009.

Dimock, George E., Jr. "The Name of Odysseus." *Essays on the Odyssey: Select Modern Criticism*, 54–72. Edited by Charles H. Taylor, Jr. Bloomington: Indiana University Press, 1963.

Dodson, Joseph R. *The "Powers" of Personification in the* Book of Wisdom *and the Letter to the Romans*. BZNW 161. Berlin: de Gruyter, 2008.

Dupertuis, Rubén R. "Bold Speech, Opposition, and Philosophical Imagery in Acts." *Engaging Early Christian History: Reading Acts in the Second Century*, 153–68. Edited by Rubén R. Dupertuis and Todd Penner. London: Routledge, 2014.

Dupertuis, Rubén R. "The Summaries in Acts 2, 4 and 5 and Greek Utopian Literary Traditions." PhD diss., Claremont Graduate University, 2005.

Dupertuis, Rubén R. and Todd Penner, eds. *Engaging Early Christian History: Reading Acts in the Second Century*. London: Routledge, 2014.

Edwards, Douglas. "The Socio-economic and Cultural Ethos of the Lower Galilee in the First Century: Implications for the Nascent Jesus Movement." *The Galilee in Late Antiquity*, 14–72. Edited by Lee I. Levine. New York: Jewish Theological Seminary of America, 1992.

Ehrman, Bart D. *How Jesus Became God: The Exaltation of a Jewish Preacher from Galilee*. San Francisco: HarperCollins, 2014.

Elter, Anton. *Donarum Pateras (Horat. Carm. 4.8)*. Programm zur Feier des Gedächtnisses des Stifters der Universität Königs Friedrich Wilhelm III. Bonn: C. Georgi, 1907.

Esposito, Stephen. *Euripides' Bacchae: Translation, Introduction, and Notes*. Focus Classical Library. Newburyport, MA: Focus, 1998.

Finkelberg, Margalit. "Canonising and Decanonising Homer." *Homer and the Bible in the Eyes of Ancient Interpreters*, 15–28. Edited by Maren R. Niehoff. JSRC 16. Leiden: Brill, 2012.

Finkelberg, Margalit. "Homer as a Foundation Text." *Homer, the Bible, and Beyond: Literary and Religious Canons in the Ancient World*, 75–96. Edited by Margalit Finkelberg and Guy G. Stromasa. JSRC 2. Leiden: Brill, 2003.

Fitzmyer, Joseph A. *The Acts of the Apostles: A New Translation with Introduction and Commentary*. AB 31. New York: Doubleday, 1998.

Freyne, Sean. "The Galileans in the Light of Josephus' *Vita*." *NTS* 26.3 (1980): 397–413.

Fridrichsen, Anton. "The Conflict of Jesus with the Unclean Spirits." *Theology* 22.129 (1931): 122–35.

Friesen, Courtney J. P. *Reading Dionysus: Euripides'* Bacchae *and the Cultural Contestations of Greeks, Jews, Romans, and Christians*. STAC 95. Tübingen: Mohr Siebeck, 2015.

Froelich, Margaret, and Thomas E. Phillips. "Throw the Blasphemer off a Cliff: Luke 4.16–30 in Light of the *Life of Aesop*." *NTS*, forthcoming.

Gibbon, Edward. "On the *Fasti* of Ovid." *The Miscellaneous Works of Edward Gibbons, Esquire: With Memoirs of His Life and Writings*, 354–58. Edited by John Lord Sheffield. Vol. 4. London: John Murray, 1814.

Gilbert, Gary. "The List of Nations in Acts 2: Roman Ideology and the Lucan Response." *JBL* 121.3 (2002): 497–529.

Glenn, Justin. "Mezentius and Polyphemus." *AJP* 92.2 (1971): 129–55.

Glenn, Justin. "The Polyphemus Myth: Its Origin and Interpretation." *GR* 25.2 (1978): 141–55.

Glenn, Justin. "Virgil's Polyphemus." *GR* 19.1 (1972): 47–59.

Grant, Robert M. "Pliny and the Christians." *HTR* 41.4 (1948): 273–74.

Gregory of Nyssa. *Select Writings and Letters of Gregory, Bishop of Nyssa*. Translated by William Moore and Henry Austin Wilson. NPNF[2] 5. 1893. Repr., Peabody, MA: Hendrickson, 1994.

Grensted, Laurence W. *A Short History of the Doctrine of the Atonement*. Manchester: Manchester University Press, 1920.

Gundry, Robert H. *Mark: A Commentary on His Apology for the Cross*. Grand Rapids: Eerdmans, 1993.

Haenchen, Ernst. *The Acts of the Apostles: A Commentary*. Oxford: Blackwell, 1971.

Halbertal, Moshe. *People of the Book: Canon, Meaning, and Authority.* Cambridge, MA: Harvard University Press, 1997.

Hernández, Pura Nieto. "Back in the Cave of the Cyclops." *AJP* 121.3 (2000): 345–66.

Herzog-Hauser, Gertrud. "Die Tendenzen der Apollonius-Biographie." *Jahrbuch der österreichischen Leo-Gesellschaft* (1930): 177–200.

Hogeterp, Albert L. A. "New Testament Greek as Popular Speech: Adolf Deissmann in Retrospect." *ZNW* 102.2 (2011): 178–200.

Hooker, Morna D. Review of *The Homeric Epics and the Gospel of Mark*, by Dennis R. MacDonald. *JTS* 53.1 (2002): 196–98.

Horsley, Richard A. *Hearing the Whole Story: The Politics of Plot in Mark's Gospel.* Louisville: Westminster John Knox, 2001.

Horsley, Richard A., and John S. Hanson. *Bandits, Prophets, and Messiahs: Popular Movements at the Time of Jesus.* Minneapolis: Winston, 1985.

Incigneri, Brian J. *The Gospel to the Romans: The Setting and Rhetoric of Mark's Gospel.* BibInt 65. Leiden: Brill, 2003.

Jackson, Howard M. "The Death of Jesus in Mark and the Miracle from the Cross." *NTS* 33.1 (1987); 16–37.

Jacobson, Howard. "Cacus and the Cyclops." *Mnemosyne* 42.1 (1989): 101–02.

Joy, C. I. David. *Mark and Its Subalterns: A Hermeneutical Paradigm for a Postcolonial Context.* London: Equinox, 2008.

Keener, Craig S. *Acts: An Exegetical Commentary.* 4 vols. Grand Rapids: Baker Academic, 2012–2015.

Kittel, Gerhard, and Gerhard Friedrich, eds. *Theological Dictionary of the New Testament.* Translated by Geoffrey W. Bromiley. 10 vols. Grand Rapids, Eerdmans, 1964–1976.

Klinghardt, Matthias. *Das älteste Evangelium und die Entstehung der kanonischen Evangelien*. 2 vols. TANZ 60. Tübingen: Francke, 2015.

Klinghardt, Matthias. "The Marcionite Gospel and the Synoptic Problem: A New Suggestion." *NovT* 50.1 (2008): 1–27.

Klinghardt, Matthias. "Marcion's Gospel and the New Testament: Catalyst or Consequence?" *NTS* 63.2 (2017): 318–23.

Klinghardt, Matthias. "Markion vs. Lukas: Plädoyer für die Wiederaufnahme eines alten Falles." *NTS* 52.4 (2006): 484–513.

Kloppenborg, John S. "Literate Media in Early Christ Groups: The Creation of a Christian Book Culture." *JECS* 22.1 (2014): 21–59.

Knox, John. *Marcion and the New Testament: An Essay in the Early History of the Canon*. Chicago: University of Chicago Press, 1942.

Kochenash, Michael. "Cornelius's Obeisance to Peter (Acts 10:25–26) and Judaea Capta Coins." *CBQ*, forthcoming.

Kochenash, Michael. "Empire without End: Juxtaposing the Kingdom of God with Rome in Luke-Acts." PhD diss., Claremont School of Theology, 2017.

Kochenash, Michael. "Political Correction: Luke's Tabitha (Acts 9:36–43), Virgil's Dido, and Cleopatra." *NovT* 60.1 (2018): 1–13.

Kochenash, Michael. "Reconsidering Luke-Acts and Virgil's *Aeneid*: Negotiating Ethnic Legacies." *Christian Origins and the New Testament in the Greco-Roman Context: Essays in Honor of Dennis R. MacDonald*, 7–38. Edited by Margaret Froelich et al. CSNTCO 1. Claremont, CA: Claremont Press, 2016.

Kochenash, Michael. "You Can't Hear 'Aeneas' without Thinking of Rome." *JBL* 136.3 (2017): 667–85.

Koester, Helmut. "On Heroes, Tombs, and Early Christianity: An Epilogue." *Flavius Philostratus*: *Heroikos*, 257–64.

Translated by Jennifer K. Berenson Maclean and Ellen Bradshaw Aitken. WGRW 1. Atlanta: Society of Biblical Literature, 2001.

Koskenniemi, Erkki. *Apollonios von Tyana in der neutestamentlichen Exegese: Forschungsbericht und Weiterführung der Diskussion*. WUNT II/61. Tübingen: Mohr Siebeck, 1994.

Kratz, Reinhard. *Rettungswunder: Motiv-, traditions- und formkritische Aufarbeitung einer biblischen Gattung*. EH 23/123. Frankfurt am Main: Peter Lang, 1979.

Lieu, Judith M. *Marcion and the Making of a Heretic: God and Scripture in the Second Century*. Cambridge: Cambridge University Press, 2015.

Lightfoot, R. H. *History and Interpretation in the Gospels*. New York: Harper, 1934.

Long, A. A. "Stoic Readings of Homer." *Homer's Ancient Readers: The Hermeneutics of Greek Epic's Earliest Exegetes*, 41–66. Edited by Robert Lamberton and John J. Keany. Princeton: Princeton University Press, 1992.

Louden, Bruce. *Homer's* Odyssey *and the Near East*. Cambridge: Cambridge University Press, 2011.

Lunn, Nicholas P. *The Original Ending of Mark: A New Case for the Authenticity of Mark 16:9–20*. Eugene: Wipf and Stock, 2014.

MacDonald, Dennis R. "A Categorization of Antetextuality in the Gospels and Acts: A Case for Luke's Imitation of Plato and Xenophon to Depict Paul as a Christian Socrates." *The Intertextuality of the Epistles: Explorations of Theory and Practice*, 211–25. Edited by Thomas L. Brodie, Dennis R. MacDonald, and Stanley E. Porter. Sheffield: Sheffield Phoenix Press, 2006.

MacDonald, Dennis R. *Christianizing Homer: The* Odyssey, Plato, *and the* Acts of Andrew. Oxford: Oxford University Press, 1994.

MacDonald, Dennis R. "Classical Greek Poetry and the Acts of the Apostles: Imitations of Euripides' *Bacchae*."

Christian Origins and Greco-Roman Culture: Social and Literary Contexts for the New Testament, 463–96. Edited by Stanley E. Porter and Andrew W. Pitts. ECHC 1. TENTS 9. Leiden: Brill 2013.

MacDonald, Dennis R. *The Dionysian Gospel: The Fourth Gospel and Euripides*. Minneapolis: Fortress, 2017.

MacDonald, Dennis R. *Does the New Testament Imitate Homer? Four Cases from the Acts of the Apostles*. New Haven: Yale University Press, 2003.

MacDonald, Dennis R. *The Gospels and Homer: Imitations of Greek Epic in Mark and Luke-Acts*. NTGL 1. Lanham, MD: Rowman & Littlefield, 2015.

MacDonald, Dennis R. *The Homeric Epics and the Gospel of Mark*. New Haven: Yale University Press, 2000.

MacDonald, Dennis R. *Luke and Vergil: Imitations of Classical Greek Literature*. NTGL 2. Lanham, MD: Rowman & Littlefield, 2015.

MacDonald, Dennis R. "Luke's Eutychus and Homer's Elpenor: Acts 20:7–12 and *Odyssey* 10–12." *JHC* 1.1 (1994): 5–24.

MacDonald, Dennis R. *My Turn: A Critique of Critics of "Mimesis Criticism."* Occasional Papers of the Institute for Antiquity and Christianity 53. Claremont, CA: Institute for Antiquity and Christianity, 2009.

MacDonald, Dennis R. *Mythologizing Jesus: From Jewish Teacher to Epic Hero*. Lanham, MD: Rowman & Littlefield, 2015.

MacDonald, Dennis R. *Two Shipwrecked Gospels: The* Logoi *of Jesus and Papias's Exposition of Logia about the Lord*. ECL 8. Atlanta: Society of Biblical Literature, 2012.

Mack, Burton L. and Vernon K. Robbins. *Patterns of Persuasion in the Gospels*. Sonoma, CA: Polebridge, 1989.

Marcus, Joel. *Mark 1–16: A New Translation with Introduction and Commentary*. 2 vols. AB 27–27A. New York: Doubleday; New Haven: Yale University Press, 2000–2009.

Marcus, Joel. "Mark—Interpreter of Paul." *NTS* 46.4 (2000): 473–87.

Martin, Michael Wade. "Defending the 'Western Non-Interpolations': The Case for an Anti-Separationist *Tendenz* in the Longer Alexandrian Readings." *JBL* 124.2 (2005): 269–94.

Martyn, J. Louis. *History and Theology in the Fourth Gospel*. 3rd ed. NTL. Louisville: Westminster John Knox, 2003.

Matthews, Shelly. "Does Dating Luke-Acts into the Second Century Affect the Q Hypothesis?" *Gospel Interpretation and the Q-Hypothesis*, 245–66. Edited by Mogens Müller and Heike Omerzu. LNTS 573. London: Bloomsbury T&T Clark, 2018.

Matthews, Shelly. *First Converts: Rich Pagan Women and the Rhetoric of Mission in Early Judaism and Christianity*. Contraversions: Jews and Other Differences. Stanford, CA: Stanford University Press, 2001.

Matthews, Shelly. *Perfect Martyr: The Stoning of Stephen and the Construction of Christian Identity*. Oxford: Oxford University Press, 2010.

Meagher, John C. *Clumsy Construction in Mark's Gospel: A Critique of Form- and Redaktionsgeschichte*. Toronto Studies in Theology 3. New York: Mellen, 1979.

Merry, W. Walter, et al. *Homer's* Odyssey. 2 vols. Oxford: Clarendon, 1886–1901.

Metzger, Bruce M. *A Textual Commentary on the Greek New Testament*. 2nd ed. Stuttgart: Deutsche Bibelgesellschaft, 1994.

Miller, Richard C. *Resurrection and Reception in Early Christianity*. Routledge Studies in Religion 44. New York: Routledge, 2015.

Morgan, Teresa. *Literate Education in the Hellenistic and Roman Worlds*. Cambridge: Cambridge University Press, 1998.

Mount, Christopher. *Pauline Christianity: Luke-Acts and the Legacy of Paul*. NovTSup 104. Leiden: Brill, 2002.

Mühlenberg, Ekkehard, ed. *Gregorii Nysseni Oratio Catechetica: Opera Dogmatica Minora, Pars IV.* Collegium Patristicum ab Academiis Gottingensi Heidelbergensi Moguntina Monacensi Institutum. Leiden: Brill, 1996.

Müller, Mogens, and Jesper Tang Nielsen, eds. *Luke's Literary Creativity.* LNTS 550. London: Bloomsbury T&T Clark, 2016.

Munk, Linda. *Devil's Mousetrap: Redemption and Colonial American Literature.* Oxford: Oxford University Press, 1997.

Mynors, R. A. B., ed. *P. Vergili Maronis Opera.* OCT. Oxford: Clarendon, 1969.

Nasrallah, Laura. "The Acts of the Apostles, Greek Cities, and Hadrian's Panhellenion." *JBL* 127.3 (2008): 533–66.

Nestle, Wilhelm. "Anklänge an Euripides in der Apostelgeschichte." *Phil* 59 (1900): 46–57.

Newton, Rick M. "The Rebirth of Odysseus." *GRBS* 25.1 (1984): 5–20.

Nock, Arthur Darby. "Notes on Ruler-Cult, I–IV." *JHS* 48.1 (1928): 21–43.

Numenius. *Fragments.* Edited by Édouard des Places. Paris: Les Belles Lettres, 2003.

O'Neill, J. C. *The Theology of Acts in Its Historical Settings.* London: SPCK, 1961.

Otis, Brooks. *Virgil: A Study in Civilized Poetry.* Oxford: Clarendon, 1964.

Parsenios, George L. *Departure and Consolation: The Johannine Farewell Discourses in Light of Greco-Roman Literature.* NovTSup 117. Leiden: Brill, 2005.

Parsenios, George L. *Rhetoric and Drama in the Johannine Lawsuit Motif.* WUNT I/258. Tübingen: Mohr Siebeck, 2010.

Parsons, Mikeal C. *Acts.* Paideia. Grand Rapids: Baker Academic, 2008.

Penner, Todd. "Reconfiguring the Rhetorical Study of Acts: Reflections on the Method in and Learning of a Progymnastic Poetics." *PRSt* 30.3 (2003): 425–39.

Pervo, Richard I. *Acts: A Commentary*. Edited by Harold W. Attridge. Hermeneia. Minneapolis: Fortress, 2009.

Pervo, Richard I. *Dating Acts: Between the Evangelists and the Apologists*. Santa Rosa, CA: Polebridge, 2006.

Phillips, Thomas E. "The Genre of Acts: Moving toward a Consensus?" *CBR* 4.3 (2006): 361–94.

Phillips, Thomas E. "How Did Paul Become a Roman 'Citizen'? Reading Acts in Light of Pliny the Younger." *Luke on Jesus, Paul and Christianity: What Did He Really Know?*, 171–89. Edited by Joseph Verheyden and John S. Kloppenborg. BTS 29. Leuven: Peeters, 2017.

Philostratus. *Apollonius of Tyana*. Edited by Christopher P. Jones. 3 vols. LCL. Cambridge, MA: Harvard University Press, 2005.

Quine, Willard Van Orman. *Word and Object*. Cambridge: MIT Press, 1960.

Reis, David M. "The Areopagus as Echo Chamber: *Mimesis* and Intertextuality in Acts." *JHC* 9.2 (2002): 259–77.

Rhoads, David, and Donald Michie. *Mark as Story: An Introduction to the Narrative of a Gospel*. Philadelphia: Fortress, 1982.

Robbins, Vernon K. "Writing as a Rhetorical Act in Plutarch and the Gospels." *Persuasive Artistry: Studies in New Testament Rhetoric in Honor of George A. Kennedy*, 157–86. Edited by Duane F. Watson. JSNTSup 50. Sheffield: JSOT, 1991.

Rohrbaugh, Richard L. "The Social Location of the Markan Audience." *Interpretation* 47.4 (1993): 380–95.

Roth, Dieter T. *The Text of Marcion's Gospel*. NTTSD 49. Leiden: Brill, 2015.

Rupp, Joseph, ed. *S. Cyrilli opera quae supersunt omnia*, vol. 2. Munich: Sumptibus Librariae Lentnerianae 1860; repr., Hildesheim: Olms, 1967.

Sandmel, Samuel. "Parallelomania." *JBL* 81.1 (1962): 1–13.
Sandnes, Karl Olav. *The Gospel 'according to Homer and Virgil': Cento and Canon*. NovTSup 138. Leiden: Brill, 2011.
Sandnes, Karl Olav. "*Imitatio Homeri*? An Appraisal of Dennis R. MacDonald's 'Mimesis Criticism.'" *JBL* 124.4 (2005): 715–32.
Sandnes, Karl Olav. "Paul and Socrates: The Aim of Paul's Areopagus Speech." *JSNT* 15.50 (1993): 13–26.
Sandt, Huub van de. "The Fate of the Gentiles in Joel and Acts 2: An Intertextual Study." *ETL* 66.1 (1990): 56–77.
Sansone, David. "Cacus and the Cyclops: An Addendum." *Mnemosyne* 44.1 (1991): 171.
Schein, Seth L. "Odysseus and Polyphemus in the *Odyssey*." *GRBS* 11.2 (1972): 73–83.
Seaford, Richard. "Thunder, Lightning and Earthquake in the *Bacchae* and the Acts of the Apostles." *What Is a God? Studies in the Nature of Greek Divinity*, 139–52. Edited by Alan B. Lloyd. London: Duckworth, 1997.
Shiner, Whitney T. "The Ambiguous Pronouncement of the Centurion and the Shrouding of Meaning in Mark." *JSNT* 22.78 (2000): 3–22.
Sider, Ronald J. "St. Paul's Understanding of the Nature and Significance of the Resurrection in 1 Corinthians XV 1–19." *NovT* 19.2 (1977): 124–41.
Smend, Friedrich. "Untersuchungen zu den Acta-Darstellungen von der Bekehrung des Paulus." *Angelos* 1 (1925): 34–45.
Smith, Dennis E., and Joseph B. Tyson, eds. *Acts and Christian Beginnings: The Acts Seminar Report*. Salem, OR: Polebridge, 2013.
Smyth, Herbert Weir. *Greek Grammar*. Revised by Gordon M. Messing. Cambridge, MA: Harvard University Press, 1956.
Solmsen, Friedrich, Reinhold Merkelbach, eds. *Hesiodi Opera*. 3rd ed. OCT. Oxford: Clarendon, 1990.

Stein, Robert H. *Studying the Synoptic Gospels: Origin and Interpretation*. 2nd ed. Grand Rapids: Baker Academic, 2001.
Sterling, Gregory E. "*Mors philosophi*: The Death of Jesus in Luke." *HTR* 94.4 (2001): 383–402.
Stowers, Stanley. "The Concept of 'Community' and the History of Early Christianity." *MTSR* 23.3 (2011): 238–56.
Streeter, B. F. *The Four Gospels: A Study of Origins, Treating of the Manuscript Tradition, Sources, Authorship, & Dates*. Rev. ed. London: Macmillan, 1936.
Swete, Henry Barclay. *The Gospel according to St. Mark: The Greek Text with Introduction, Notes and Indices*. Grand Rapids: Eerdmans, 1956.
Theissen, Gerd. *Social Reality and the Early Christians: Theology, Ethics and the World of the New Testament*. Edinburgh: T&T Clark, 1993.
Tyson, Joseph B. "The Date of Acts: A Reconsideration." *Forum* n.s. 5.1 (2002): 33–51.
Tyson, Joseph B. *Marcion and Luke-Acts: A Defining Struggle*. Columbia: University of South Carolina Press, 2014.
Tyson, Joseph B. "Why Dates Matter: The Case of the Acts of the Apostles." *The Fourth R* 18.2 (2005): 8–14.
Vögeli, Alfred. "Lukas und Euripides." *TZ* 9 (1953): 415–38.
Wahlde, Urban C. von. *The Gospel and Letters of John*. 3 vols. ECC. Grand Rapids: Eerdmans, 2010.
Watson, David F. "The *Life of Aesop* and the Gospel of Mark: Two Ancient Approaches to Elite Values." *JBL* 129.4 (2010): 699–716.
Watts, Rikki E. *Isaiah's New Exodus in Mark*. WUNT II/88. Tübingen: Mohr Siebeck, 1997.
Weaver, John B. *Plots of Epiphany: Prison Escape in the Acts of the Apostles*. BZNW 131. Berlin: de Gruyter, 2004.
Weinreich, Otto. *Gebet und Wunder: Zwei Abhandlungen zur Religions- und Literaturgeschichte in Religionsgeschichtliche*

Studien. Darmstadt: Wissenschaftliche Buchgesellschaft, 1968.
Wellhausen, Julius. *Das Evangelium Marci übersetzt und erklärt*. 2nd ed. Berlin: Reimer, 1903.
Whitmarsh, Tim. *Greek Literature and the Roman Empire: The Politics of Imitation*. Oxford: Oxford University Press, 2001.
Williams, Michael. *Rethinking "Gnosticism": An Argument for Dismantling a Dubious Category*. Princeton: Princeton University Press, 1996.
Winn, Adam. *Mark and the Elijah-Elisha Narrative: Considering the Practice of Greco-Roman Imitation in the Search for Markan Source Material*. Eugene: Wipf and Stock, 2010.
Wischmeyer, Oda, David C. Sim, and Ian J. Elmer, eds. *Paul and Mark: Comparative Essays Part I: Two Authors at the Beginning of Christianity*. BZNW 198. Berlin: de Gruyter, 2014.
Witherington, Ben, III. *The Gospel of Mark: A Socio-Rhetorical Commentary*. Grand Rapids: Eerdmans, 2001.
Wright, N. T. *The Resurrection of the Son of God*. Christian Origins and the Question of God 3. Minneapolis: Fortress, 2003.
Zeitlin, Froma I. "Visions and Revisions of Homer." *Being Greek under Rome: Cultural Identity, the Second Sophistic and the Development of Empire*, 195–266. Edited by Simon Goldhill. Cambridge: Cambridge University Press, 2001.
Ziegler, Detlef. *Dionysos in der Apostelgeschichte – eine intertextuelle Lektüre*. Religion und Biographie 18. Berlin: Lit, 2008.

Index of Scriptural References

Genesis
  1:27, 106
  11:1–9, 114
  2:24, 106
Deuteronomy
  24:1–4, 106
1 Samuel
  16:14, 86
Daniel
  12:2, 85
  7, 85
  7:24–25, 85
  7:8, 85
  8:9–14, 85
  9:26–27, 85
Joel
  2:28, 114
  2:28–32, 119
Matthew
  27:15, 132
  27:53, 79
  27:54, 84
  28:11–15, 90
  8:5–13, 58

Mark
  1:1, 83
  1:11, 82
  1:12–13, 82
  1:16–20, 28
  1:21–28, 82
  1:23–26, 28
  1:24, 75, 82, 83
  1:28, 28
  1:32–34, 28
  1:34, 82
  1:39, 28
  1:40, 28
  1:45, 28
  1:6, 29
  10, 111
  10:1, 132
  10:1–12, 106–7
  10:14–15, 29
  10:17–23, 28
  10:29–30, 29
  10:34, 92, 93
  10:42–45, 29
  10:45, 82, 85, 93, 95
  10:46–52, 28
  10:46–62, 98

11:27–33, 29
12:13–17, 28
12:1–9, 28
12:38–39, 29
12:40–44, 28
12:42, 29
13:14, 85
13:16, 28
13:19, 85
13:2, 85
13:24–26, 93
13:32, 83
13:34–36, 28
14:22–24, 94
14:23–24, 83
14:27–31, 90
14:28, 90, 92
14:29–31, 90
14:3, 28
14:35–36, 93
14:36, 83
14:51–52, 89
14:53–65, 94
14:61, 83
15:1–5, 94
15:27, 28
15:34, 86, 93
15:37, 83, 84, 86
15:38, 83
15:39, 82–85, 83, 86
15:43–45, 102

15:45–46, 82
15:46, 73, 79
16:1, 55
16:3, 78
16:4, 79
16:4–6, 86
16:5–7, 89
16:6, 89
16:7, 90
16:8, 87
2:1–12, 28
2:15, 28
3:10, 28
3:11, 82, 83
3:11–12, 28
3:15, 28
3:1–5, 28
3:22, 28
3:22–30, 82
3:27, 82, 85, 95
3:31, 29
3:7, 28
4:1, 28
4:19, 29
4:2–10, 28
4:26–32, 28
5:1, 73
5:10–12, 76
5:1–20, 28, 82
5:13, 76
5:14–17, 74

5:15, 74
5:19, 78
5:2, 73
5:20, 78
5:21, 28
5:24, 28
5:25–34, 28
5:3, 73
5:3–4, 74
5:6, 84
5:7, 77, 83, 84, 86
5:9, 75
6, 21
6:13, 28
6:14–29, 94
6:24–30, 82
6:3, 28
6:33–34, 28
6:53–56, 28
6:6, 28
6:7, 82
7:22, 29
7:25–30, 28
7:31-37, 31
7:32–35, 28
8:1–9, 28
8:22–26, 28, 31, 98
8:31, 92, 93
8:31–9:1, 93
9:14, 28
9:14–29, 82

9:15–27, 28
9:31, 92, 93
9:42, 28
9:7, 82, 83
9:9, 92

Luke
  1:5-25, 63
  1:57-80, 63
  10:38–39, 55
  1–2, 58
  12:37–38, 55
  1–3, 63
  13:22–30, 126
  14:12–24, 126
  16:20a, 55
  18:35–19:10, 46
  19:1–10, 126
  19:1-2, 65
  19:8-10, 65
  2:25–35, 64
  2:28–35, 126
  2:41–52, 64
  22:24–27, 55
  22:3a, 56
  22–23, 23
  23, 58, 64
  23:27ff, 64
  23:34a, 56
  23:43, 56
  23:53, 79
  24, 90

24:1, 55
24:10, 55
24:12, 56
24:13–35, 58, 102
24:36, 56
24:37–39, 55
24:37–43, 64
24:40, 56
24:42-43, 57
24:44–53, 58
24:49–52, 64
3:1-14, 63
3:20b, 56
3:22, 64
4:16–30, 126, 131–32
4:29–30, 55, 65
4:9b–10, 56
5:1–11, 61, 65
6:22–23, 132
7:1–10, 58
7:37–38, 55
8:1–3, 65

John
1:49, 51b, 56
10:39, 55, 66
11:1–2, 55
13:1–20, 47
13:16, 55
13:27, 56
13:3–5, 12–17, 55
13–17, 47

14:27, 56
15, 47
18:19–21, 63
18:20–21, 57, 63
18:22–23, 57
20:1, 55
20:17, 25, 27, 55
20:19, 21, 26, 56
20:20, 56
20:24–29, 102
20:3, 11, 56
20:31, 41
20–21, 90
21, 47
21:12, 15, 57
21:3–11, 61
3:24, 56
4:46b–54, 58
6, 47
8:58b–59, 55, 66

Acts
1:8, 114
10:1–11:18, 126
10–11, 23
12:5–11, 136
13:14, 131
13:4–12, 142
13:5, 131
13:50, 138, 139
14:1, 131
16, 46

16:11–12, 133
16:13–40, 134–35
16:16–24, 135–37
16:7, 131
17:10, 131
17:10–15, 126, 140
17:1–10, 23
17:12, 126, 138, 139, 142
17:1–2, 131
17:13, 140
17:1–4, 127
17:15, 130
17:16, 121
17:17, 131
17:1–9, 125, 131, 140
17:2–3, 130
17:27, 121
17:32a, 121
17:4, 126, 138, 142
17:5, 130, 139
17:5–10, 127
17:5–9, 128
17:6, 130
17:6–7, 139
17:7, 130
17–28, 22
18:19, 131
18:4, 131
19:8, 131
2, 119
2:11, 118

2:13, 120
2:18, 119
2:42, 120
2:42–47, 115, 119
2:44, 120
2:47, 120
2:8, 118
2:9–11, 114
20:25, 19
21:27–31, 126
23:2–4, 57
24:19–21, 57
2–5, 46
27, 23
28, 114
4, 119
4:32, 120
5, 119
5:14, 138
5:17–32, 136
8:12, 138
9:1–19a, 46

Romans
  5–7, 85

1 Corinthians
  15, 65, 90
  15:20–23, 79
  15:3–7, 87
  15:4, 88
  15:54–55, 85

Revelation
 1:10–22:7, 53
 13:1–9, 85

Index of Modern Authors[1]

Adams, S. A., 18

Allen, T. W., 73

Anderson, G., 109

Attridge, H., 43, 127

Aulén, G., 83, 96

Barrett, C. K., 128, 136

Baur, F. C., 98

Becker, Engberg-Pedersen, and Müller, 87

BeDuhn, J. D., 59

Belo, F., 29

Bilby, M. G., 15, 22, 54, 62, 110, 147, 149, 151

Blumenthal, C., 126

Bonner, C., 75

Boter, G., 99

Brant, J. A., 43

Brodie, T. L., 9

Brookins, T. A., 17

Bruce, F. F., 115

---

[1] As this volume is dedicated to interacting with the work of Dennis R. MacDonald, it is only a slight exaggeration to say that citations to his work appear on nearly every page. We have therefore chosen not to include him in the index, and we instead encourage our readers to familiarize themselves with his corpus on its own terms and through each of the essays presented in this volume.

Bultmann, R., 86
Busch, A., 106, 108, 155
Carhart, R., 20, 122
Carter, W., 84
Collins, A. Y., 76, 83, 89
Conzelmann, H., 139
Crossan, J. D., 88
D'Angelo, M. R., 54
Danker, F. W., 85
Dimock, G. E. Jr., 86
Dodson, J. R., 85
Dupertuis and Penner, 54
Dupertuis, R. R., 20, 119, 122
Edwards, D., 29
Ehrman, B. D., 88
Elter, A., 40
Esposito, S., 133
Finkelberg, M., 103
Fitzmyer, J. A., 139
Freyne, S., 29
Fridrichsen, A., 82
Friesen, C. J. P., 61, 127
Froelich and Phillips, 132
Gibbon, E., 103
Gilbert, G., 114
Glenn, J., 80, 81, 92
Grant, R. M., 61, 117

Grensted, L. W., 97
Gundry, R. H., 75, 84, 92
Haenchen, E., 139
Halbertal, M., 104
Hernández, P. N., 86, 92
Herzog-Hauser, Gertud, 98
Hogeterp, A., 30
Hooker, M. D., 110
Horsley and Hanson, 28
Horsley, R. A., 29
Incigneri, B. J., 85
Jackson, H. M., 83
Jacobson, H., 81
Joy, C. I. D., 28
Keener, C. S., 114, 128, 131
Klinghardt, M., 54, 60
Kloppenborg, J. S., 54
Knox, J., 54, 59
Kochenash, M., 12, 23, 26, 45, 46, 116, 132, 143, 148, 151, 152
Koester, H., 91
Koskenniemi, E., 98, 102
Kratz, R., 127
Lieu, J. M., 59
Lightfoot, R. H., 76
Long, A. A., 103
Louden, B., 25
Lunn, N. P., 87

Mack and Robbins, 17

Marcus, J., 30, 33, 76, 84, 86, 87

Martin, J. L., 48

Martin, M. W., 56

Matthews, S., 54, 56, 62, 134

Meagher, J. C., 30

Merry, W., 73, 74

Metzger, B. M., 79

Michaelis, W., 137

Miller, R. C., 12, 147, 149

Morgan, T., 116

Mount, C., 54

Mühlenberg, E., 95

Müller and Nielsen, 18

Munk, L., 96

Mynors, R. A. B., 80

Nasrallah, L., 54

Nestle, W., 126

Newton, R. M., 87

Nock, A. D., 40

O'Neill, J. C., 54

Otis, B., 81

Park, C. S., 23, 148

Park, I., 15, 23, 46, 61, 127, 155

Parsenios, G., 43

Parsons, M. C., 53

Penner, T., 17

Pervo, R. I., 53, 128, 130

Phillips, T. E., 54, 62, 113

Quine, W. V. O., 104

Reis, D. M., 122

Rhoads and Michie, 26

Robbins, V. K., 17

Rohrbaugh, R. L., 29

Roth, D. T., 59

Rupp, J., 96

Sandmel, S., 8

Sandnes, K. O., 24, 110, 121

Sandt, H. van de, 114

Sansone, D., 81

Schein, S. L., 74, 86

Seaford, R., 127

Shiner, W. T., 83

Sider, R. J., 88

Smend, F., 126

Smith and Tyson, 54

Smith, K. H., 18, 145

Smyth, H. W., 74

Solmsen, F., 92

Stein, R. H., 89

Sterling, G. E., 64

Stowers, S., 48

Streeter, B. F., 88

Swete, H. B., 30

Theissen, G., 29

Tyson, J. B., 54, 60

Van Dijk, Gert-Jan, 98

Vögeli, A., 127

Wahlde, U. C. von, 44

Watson, D. F., 29, 30, 31

Watts, R. E., 76

Weaver, J. B., 127

Weinreich, O., 126

Wellhausen, J., 75

Whitmarsh, T., 44

Williams, M., 109

Winn, A., 103, 109

Wischmeyer, Sim, and Elmer, 87

Witherington, B. III, 29

Wright, N. T., 88

Zeitlin, F. I., 104

Ziegler, D., 126, 135

Index of Citations to Ancient Works

Aeschylus
Eumenides
24–34, 135
Apollodorus
Library
1.2, 92
Apollonius of Rhodes
Argonautica
1.5–17, 129
1.6–7, 129
Cicero
De natura deorum
2.24, 40
Cyril of Jerusalem
Catechetical Lectures
12.15, 96
Euripides
Bacchae
1–2, 133
13–42, 133
215–262, 135
221–22, 118
298–301, 118
443–50, 136
5, 135
509–10, 136
516–18, 136
55–56, 134

576–603, 136
615–22, 136
627–31, 137
635, 137
Gregory of Nyssa
Oratio Catechetica
65 M [24], 96
Gregory the Great
Moralia
33.7, 96
Hesiod
Theogonia
453–506, 91
485–92, 93
493–96, 92
Homer
Iliad
15.624, 33
18.336–37, 108
23.175–76, 108
6.146, 33
Odyssey
10.135–465, 76
9.105–07, 73
9.114, 73
9.182, 73
9.240–41, 79
9.240–43, 79
9.288–93, 80

9.345–74, 93
9.347–49, 94
9.366–67, 74
9.371–74, 92
9.399–412, 73
9.405, 75
9.408, 74
9.411, 73
9.413–63, 76
9.502–05, 78
9.526–36, 78

Horace
- *Ars poetica*
  - 359, 18

Jerome
- *Vita S. Hilarionis eremitae*
  - 23, 76

John of Damascus
- *De fide orthodoxa*
  - 3.27, 96

Josephus
- *Antiquitates judaicae*
  - 18.116–119, 21

Justin
- *Dialogue with Trypho*
  - 8.1, 121

Macarius Magnes
- *Apocriticus*
  - 3.4, 76

Numenius
- Fr. 30 Des Places, 110

Origen
- *Contra Celsum*
  - I.9, 121

Philo
- *de Ebrietate*
  - 146, 118

Philostratus
- *Heroicus*
  - 33, 105
  - 48.5–10, 108
  - 49, 108
- *Life of Apollonius*
  - 4.16, 105
  - 4.16.6, 105
  - 4.20, 98
  - 4.36, 99, 100
  - 4.36.3, 99
  - 4.44, 100
  - 4.44.1, 100
  - 4.44.2, 100
  - 4.44.3, 100
  - 4.44.4, 100
  - 7.28, 99
  - 7.28.2, 101
  - 7.28.3, 101
  - 8.11–12, 101
  - 8.8, 101

Pindar
- *Pythian Odes*
  - 4.156–68, 129
  - 4.71–119, 129
  - 4.71–78, 129

Pliny the Younger
- 10.96, 61, 117, 121

Ptolemy

Letter to Flora
    33.4.4–10, 107

Theocritus
Idylls
    6 and 11, 80

Valerius Flaccus
Argonautica
    1.22–63, 129
    1.26–30, 129

Vergil
Aeneid
    10.185–307, 81
    12.845–86, 81
    3.621–27, 80
    3.672–74, 80
    3.675–81, 80
    6.570–72, 81
    7.323–551, 81
    8.481–93, 81

www.ingramcontent.com/pod-product-compliance
Lightning Source LLC
Chambersburg PA
CBHW070536170426
43200CB00011B/2441